The events and conversations in this book have been set down to the best of the author's ability, although some names and details have been changed to protect the privacy of individuals.

ISBN: 978-0-578-59539-9
Library of Congress Control Number: 2019916459

Edited by Michelle LeRoy
Cover and book design by David Miles

Printed in the United States

Icons and graphic elements licensed from the following Shutterstock.com artists: popcic, Alexander Ryabintsev. davooda, TheModernCanvas, musmellow, pambudi, sinausabtu, Maxim Cherednichenko, Set Line Vector Icon, Noegraha Rian, DStarky, Cube29, Skeleton Icon, Colorlife, Benn Beckman, Motorama, justone, nani888, MicroOne, Artverich, Bukhavets Mikhail, and T0RI.

First Edition

HIKING MY

feelings

STEPPING INTO
THE HEALING POWER
OF NATURE

SYDNEY WILLIAMS

DEDICATION

This book is dedicated to the survivors of - and the families affected by - generational trauma.

I hold the vision of our collective healing with every breath I take, every keystroke, and every word that crosses my lips. I hope you find what you're seeking within these pages, and I wish you nothing but health, love, wellness, and prosperity on your healing journey.

CONTENTS

ACKNOWLEDGMENTS

I'm childfree by choice, and this book is the closest I'll come to the birthing process. They say it takes a village to raise a child, and this book wouldn't be possible without a whole cast of characters, some of whom make an appearance within the pages that follow.

To my adventure buddy for life, Barry - thank you for seeing me and for holding the vision of the woman I always knew I could become. When you taught me how to save my own life, I knew my world was forever changed. When it comes to sickness and health, good times and bad, we've seen it all. The stuff we've experienced as individuals and together as a couple since we met could derail your average human, but every time we get knocked down, we keep getting back up. After this journey, I know that I am capable, strong, unfuckwithable, and oozing with love to share with the world. Thank you for reminding me that my ability to feel things intensely is my superpower. Thank you for being my rock, my best friend, my partner in everything. I love you and although I know in my heart of hearts that we've been together for lifetimes before this one, I'm really digging what we've got going on, and there's nobody else I'd rather hike through life with than you. Thank you for holding up the mirror, thank you for walking by my side, and thank you for always having my back. I trusted you before I could trust myself, and I wake up every morning grateful for the ability to see myself the way you've always seen me. You're the best teammate I've ever had, and I'm proud to wear this jersey. #sameteam

Michelle, you are a gift. I don't know who I would be without you in my life. Thank you for being on this journey with me - from our early days performing as 'munks and mice at the happiest place on earth, on the morning my life changed forever, to the first talk I gave where you sat in the front row radiating your positive energy, to the energy you've poured into this book - I couldn't have done this without you, and though this story had a tragic beginning, writing it with you by my side has been one of the happiest endings. You rock my face.

Brandi, I'm sorry I didn't tell you sooner. You were the first friend I made after my world came crumbling down and I didn't want you to think I was broken. I didn't know how much of an impact you have made on me until I met your daughter and heard how you speak to her. Serua is the luckiest girl in the whole wide world to have you in her corner. Thank you for always showing up and being exactly who you are, without apology. It's something I've always admired about you and strive to do more of myself.

Kat, I quite literally might not have ever gotten to the point where I felt comfortable talking about what happened to me if I never met you. The first memory I have of you is when you rolled into the skydiving center with your "Jeans for Justice" crew - bringing awareness to sexual assault as you chucked yourself out of a plane. My life is immeasurably better with you in it. Thank you for being my first text and phone call for so many pivotal moments, for always asking how you can support me when I'm in the middle of a trauma tornado, and for inviting me to crash the party in Paris. You inspire me endlessly and you are the epitome of sisterhood. Thank you for helping me find, claim, and own my bright and shiny.

Christine, thank you for the GIF parades before my talks, for always making me laugh, and for talking me off the ledge time and time again since that fateful day that we met in the bathroom. You're my Flava Flav. We will hike this island together, and when we get to the top of Blackjack - definitely not sweaty, dirty, or crying - we will celebrate with a single avocado.

Aaron and Melanie, thank you for seeing me, celebrating me, loving me, holding me, and supporting me in everything I set my mind to. Thank you for opening your hearts and home to us and providing a warm, loving, comforting, and peaceful place for me to write the majority of this book. I would not be the woman I am today without you both - thank you for believing my story, affirming my lived experience, and showing me what unconditional love looks like. Four, out.

To Lydia and Howard, thank you for creating this beautiful soul that is Barry. Without your son, I would not be here today. He makes me want to be the best version of myself, and he encourages me to keep sharing, keep speaking up, and keep pushing my own internalized limits. When I'm with him, I feel like anything is possible; because it is. Thank you for being some of our biggest cheerleaders, and for helping make this book a reality for me. Your support, encouragement, and unwavering faith in what we're building has been instrumental in keeping this train on the tracks. Thank you from the bottom of my heart.

Linda, thank you for bringing Adam into this world. I would prefer that he was still here with us, hiking, exploring, jumping, making a lasting impression on everyone around him, of course. In his absence, I found the strength I didn't know I had. In losing him, I gained a second mom, a friend, and a confidant. You are always on my mind and in my heart, and I hope you know just how much he meant to me, and to Barry. Thank you for continuing to be such a positive force in my life and for sprinkling little hints of Adam in each of our interactions. This book would not be possible without Adam's influence, and I am forever grateful for the time we did share, albeit all too short.

Hannah and Travis, thank you for offering notes on my talk early on in this process - your vulnerability around that table shifted the way I see this work, and I'm so grateful for your willingness to share. Thank you for helping me see that my body isn't the barrier to success in my athletic pursuits, and for helping me calm my mind in the aftermath of my skydiving career. Thank you for opening your hearts and home to us when our tour got rerouted and for being such excellent human beings. The world is better with people like you in it, and now the world will know that we need more than band-aids for our trauma.

Talia, witnessing your growth since we met has been one of the most beautiful privileges of my life. Thank you for so fearlessly sharing your story with me, for giving me language to help articulate what I experienced early in life, and for seeing me and cheering me on. As you continue to crush ultra-marathons, trail running races, and general life events, I continue to draw inspiration from how unapologetically you are claiming your space, and I aspire to continue to do the same.

Ash, thank you for showing up for that first talk. Thank you for asking the hard questions. Thank you for joining us on our first group hike. You inspire me to be a better human, and your willingness to go the extra mile to support everything we're building and make sure we are taken care of while we build it is humbling. Thank you for helping me see I am worthy of support.

Becca, thank you for being unafraid to talk about your feelings on the internet. If you kept your hiking and your feelings to yourself, I likely wouldn't have had the opportunity to connect with you, hike in Reno with you, or tap into your gorgeous brain to wrap my head around some of the things I'm feeling as we build this plane while we fly it. Thank you for jumping on the hashtag, for supporting everything we're doing here, and for being you. #Lifetimes.

Travis and Pete, thank you for giving me a space to explore the "woo-woo" side of what happened across that island. Before giving the talk for the first time, I knew a lot of the language but hadn't felt it land with me yet. What started as a podcast interview blossomed into one of the most beautiful relationships that Barry and I have ever found in two humans, and we are so thankful for your support, and for asking *what is this process, Hiking My Feelings?"* Without that question, I might not have had the courage to look back and dissect my experience and really come to understand how spending time on the trail helped me heal my mind and body. Thank you for challenging me and thank you for teaching me how to receive.

To everyone who has supported the tour, attended a talk, or hiked with us so far, thank you for showing up. For yourselves, for us, for the greater good. This work isn't possible without you, and I am so grateful to call you my chosen family.

WELCOME TO THE CAMPFIRE

Hey there. Come sit next to me around the campfire, it's story time.
Over the course of our time together within these pages, I'm
going to share stories from the two hikes I did on the Trans-Catalina Trail (TCT): a 38.5-mile trail that spans across Catalina Island, off the coast of Los Angeles, California. My husband and I embarked on the first hike in December 2016, and the second trip in June 2018 to celebrate my 33rd birthday.

I'm not a professional hiker. In fact, that first hike on the TCT was my first backpacking trip. I don't have thousands of miles under my belt, I haven't (yet) completed any of the long scenic trails like the Pacific Crest Trail or Appalachian Trail. I'm a Midwest transplant who fell in love with hiking when I moved to Southern California.

I'm not a doctor. I'm not a therapist. I'm a woman with some stories to share about how hiking helped me heal my mind and body from trauma and disease. Before we get too far into this, I want to encourage you to read this book with an open heart and an open mind. My story is complex, and I'd be willing to bet yours is too, that's why you picked up this book. Since we're all walking around with our own lived experiences and can be triggered by a whole host of things, I want you to know that in these pages, I'll be sharing about how I moved through toxic relationships, verbal and emotional abuse, suicide, cancer, sudden death, chronic illness, and sexual assault, to name a few.

I also talk about how I almost shit my pants on the trail, so it's not all doom and gloom. I promise this story ends on a high note.

That said, when it comes to my life and the things I've survived, I ask the hard questions. I dig deep. And for some folks, that can be a lot.

So, if at any point you find yourself feeling some type of way while reading or listening to this book, I invite you to grab a piece of paper, your trusty journal, or just sit and think about these questions:

> ✓ What am I feeling right now?
> ✓ Where do I feel it in my body?
> ✓ Can I remember the last time I felt this way? What caused the feeling then?

That's all. You don't have to wax poetic about the feeling, I'm not going to ask you sit with the discomfort for too long, I simply want you to acknowledge what you feel and where you feel it.

Ultimately, take what works for you and leave the rest.

Before we jump into the story of how these hikes helped me heal my mind and body, I want to share a bit about who I was before I started hiking.

To set the stage here and paint a picture of how I grew up and found my way through this world, I'm one of those *Millennials* that everyone keeps talking about. I credit my sister from another mister whom I've never met, comedian Iliza Schlesinger, for coining the term "Elder Millennial".

My first cassette tape was Michael Jackson's "Black or White", which I listened to obsessively on the way to and from gymnastics practice. I played Oregon Trail in the computer lab at school, and when my family got that first AOL disc in the mail, I was hooked and started communicating with people from all over the world in AOL chat rooms. I made it through most of high school before cell phones were available to the public, and my Nokia had several different candy shell cases. I was one of the last generations of children to grow up with their lives documented in actual photographs and poorly shot home movies, instead of on the internet.

I was raised in Overland Park, a suburb of Kansas City, Kansas. The county I grew up in was called "The Bubble" and though the majority of people I went to school with had wealthy parents, my family was not. My dad worked in the restaurant industry before I was born, then transitioned to newspaper carrier for the Kansas City Star. Newspaper Carrier is a modern term for "paperboy" and my father had a big route close to where we lived, with thousands of customers. His operation at its peak required two Ford Econoline vans and a team of two other drivers who would rotate. We helped out as soon as we were old enough to lift a bundle of newspapers and working nights with my dad on the weekends was how I earned my allowance and started to pay for college. My mom worked for the same hospital system the entire time we lived in Kansas – she started as a volunteer and worked her way up into the administrative side of things over the years.

My idea of being outdoorsy was occasional trips to the community pool and riding bikes around the neighborhood, as there wasn't a lot of outdoor recreation available to me. We didn't have a ranch, so I didn't have a ton of land to explore. We didn't have a lake house, so I didn't know anything about water sports. We didn't have a cabin in Colorado like some of my friends did, so I didn't know anything about snow sports. I grew up engrossed in gymnastics, dance classes, and Pop Warner cheerleading, which eventually led me to join a traveling competitive all-star cheerleading team, landing spots on the freshman, junior varsity, and varsity squads in high school.

After high school, my cheerleading career ended. I'd entertained dreams of cheering in college, but I was a base, not a flyer, and it was my understanding (and assumption) that big girls like me wouldn't ever make it on a co-ed team. My mom tried to shield me from the embarrassment I would surely feel as the bigger girl on a team that sported cropped tops with the midriff exposed. So, when I got accepted to the University of Kansas and wanted to have a team experience of some sort, cheerleading wasn't it.

At orientation, I discovered the Women's Rowing team. Growing up, I dabbled in volleyball, basketball, and track in middle school, and was a manager on the lacrosse team my senior year, but that was about it for sports outside of cheerleading. I walked on to an NCAA Division 1 athletic team at one of the best sports schools in the country.

We'd run up and down the bleachers at the football stadium at ungodly hours in the morning for conditioning practice. I'd hate it while we were doing it, and sometimes I'd work so hard I'd throw up. But after the nausea subsided and once my legs stopped shaking, my mind was clear. On the Kansas River and running around Lawrence, I got my first taste for extremely difficult physical activity in the outdoors and how it can help me clear my mind.

I rowed for one season at the University of Kansas, and that year changed my life. I moved to Florida with my parents during spring break of my sophomore year and took a gap year working at Walt Disney World as a costumed character in the parks and as a server in a local restaurant. During that gap year, I also made my first skydive. When I landed, I shouted, "I want to be an instructor someday!" When I got home and shared this with my parents, it was a hard "no" – they said I needed to go back to college. Once I qualified for in-state tuition, I resumed my coursework at Valencia Community College, then was accepted at the University of South Florida where I would finish my degree.

After college, I moved to Chicago for my first grownup job – an internship at a global public relations firm. It was a 16-week program and employment after the internship wasn't guaranteed. I didn't care – I was moving to Chicago and I'd figure it out if I didn't get hired. When I was in college, I had been bartending at a steakhouse in Tampa to pay for everything my student loans couldn't cover, so I figured I could always get a restaurant job in Chicago if I had to. I made one visit to the Windy City, rented an apartment, flew back home to Florida, sold all my stuff, and moved to Chicago with what could fit in my Honda Civic Hybrid.

I ended up getting hired by that firm and my life was a dream. I felt like the Midwestern version of Carrie Bradshaw (Sarah Jessica Parker's character from HBO's "Sex and the City"), but I was making $10 an hour so there were no Manolos for this former Jayhawk. I had my own studio apartment and if I looked out the window with my whole left side pressed against the glass and craning my neck, I could see Lake Michigan. *So much for a lake view*. I was writing a ton, and I had a great job at a fancy agency with world famous clients. My first account? I was writing tweets and interacting with fans of the Oscar Mayer Wienermobile on Twitter. Yep, @Wienermobile was my job. I worked on other prestigious accounts with some brilliant people and felt highly valued. And yet, I still felt like a piece of me was missing.

When I went to Austin to speak at South by Southwest (SXSW), another speaker at the conference invited some people to go skydiving with him. A few friends and I joined him, and I made my second skydive. For the minute I was in freefall, I was in a total state of bliss. I wasn't worrying about client deadlines, I wasn't checking email, I was just me, fully present, and falling toward an oncoming planet at 120 miles per hour. When I got home from the conference, I started researching what it would take to learn how to skydive by myself. The speaker who invited us to jump with him was a licensed skydiver, and he frequently went skydiving before, during, or after business trips. I was traveling a lot for work and I thought this could be a really cool way to see the world. I ended up scheduling another skydive at a drop zone west of Chicago and after I landed from that jump, I signed up for their student training program.

After I earned my skydiving license, I started dating Barry. He was my skydiving instructor and had a strict "no dating students" rule. Don't worry, I'll tell you all about how we met, fell in love, and eventually got married. For now, just know that I started skydiving in June, and by September, I was interviewing for jobs in Austin, Texas so I could skydive year-round.

I accepted a position in Austin and I call it my "semester abroad" because I quickly realized I wasn't cut out for this lifestyle – I wanted to work in the skydiving industry. I talked to the owner at the facility where I learned how to skydive and when he asked how I was liking Texas, I said flat out "well, I'd rather come back to Illinois in the spring and run your events and marketing."

He asked me how much money I'd need to make the move and how much I'd need to make per month, and we worked it out. I quit my job, sold everything I owned, sublet my apartment, and prepared to move back to Illinois with what I could fit in my Civic, once again. After I spoke at SXSW in 2011, I moved back to Illinois to work in the skydiving industry full-time. I earned my coach rating that first year, I started some new events on the drop zone, and Barry and I were a power couple in the sport. I even got my own column in Blue Skies Magazine. Life was so, so good.

The drop zone closed in the winter – jumping in the snow is no fun – so we knew we would need to move again at the end of the season. We were looking for winter work when a drop zone owner from California started coaching some skydivers at our facility. I had heard his marketing person was leaving so this could be perfect. I could do events, public relations, and marketing, and Barry could be an instructor and take a break from running a skydiving school.

I introduced myself to the coach from California and told him I was looking for opportunities during the winter months. I mentioned that I heard his marketing person was leaving, and that I'd love to be considered for the position. I shared my dreams of being a World Champion skydiver and my aspirations to give back to the sport that so beautifully changed my life. He said he didn't hire seasonal employees and that we'd have to move to California and live there all year. *Twist my arm.* Over dinner later that week, he offered me the position and invited me out to California for their biggest event of the year so I could see their business at its best – all expenses paid.

I said yes and flew out to California and fell in love. Between the mountains, the ocean, and the dry heat compared to swampy Illinois summers, my Southern California dreams were coming true. Fancy cars, movie stars, swimming pools, it was everything "The OC" and "The Hills" had promised when I was growing up, watching those shows in my parent's basement in Kansas. When I got back to Illinois, we only had a few weeks before it was time to move. Once again, Barry and I were selling everything we owned, only taking what could fit in my Civic – two humans, all of our skydiving gear, our Puggle, Jezebel, and some clothes.

When we got to California, we didn't know anyone, and we didn't have anything lined up for housing. Skydivers are special people and we take care of each other. By the end of that first day, we had a room to stay in. It was just a mattress on the ground, but we didn't care. All of our time was spent on the drop zone, so all we needed was a closet for some clothes, a shelf in the fridge, and a place to lay our heads at night.

Once we got settled in, I started my training as a competitive skydiver. The owner of the facility was now my boss, and part of my job offer was free jumps and free coaching. Someday I'll write a book about the skydiving chapter of my life, but for now, just know that it radically transformed the way I see myself, the way I see the world, and introduced me to the man who would eventually become my husband.

When we moved to Southern California, we also started doing day hikes and camping trips at Joshua Tree National Park. The hiking season was super short in the high desert because it was really hot for most of the year. We only hiked in the winter and that was only on days when we couldn't skydive. Yet, I loved it. The important things in my life were quite simple: my relationship with Barry came first, my job was second, skydiving was third, and hiking and spending time outdoors – although I didn't get to do it as frequently as I wanted to – was fourth.

Nothing else could fit on my plate. Nothing else mattered. I was living the dream – I was competing with my skydiving team, I was married to my best friend, I had just hosted the best event of my life, and now, it was time for the nice weather of the winter season and a slower pace. Before we jump into the hikes themselves and all the lessons learned along the way, I want you to understand what led me to the Trans-Catalina Trail to begin with. In short, I had just survived two of the hardest years of my life.

Let's jump back to January 2014, in my kitchen at our house in Lake Elsinore, California. That's where the story really starts.

CHAPTER 1

YOU ONLY
GET SO MANY
SUNSETS

"Sydney?" my husband Barry called out as he was making his way down the narrow hallway from our bedroom toward the kitchen.

Our Puggle, Jezebel, was following closely behind. She made a racket as she trotted behind him, her nails tapping on the linoleum. I made a mental note to trim her nails on our next day off.

I was mindlessly scanning the contents of the refrigerator, trying to find something to eat before we went to work.

"Yeah?" I responded, still looking through the fridge.

"I have some bad news," he paused.

I held my breath, feeling time slow down and my chest start to tighten as I waited for him to finish. The pause felt like an entire lifetime, adrenaline coursing through my veins.

"Chris killed himself," he continued.

Time stood still. Everything moved in slow motion. I was holding my breath, but now I felt like I couldn't breathe at all. I stood up straight and closed the refrigerator door, feeling the cold air whoosh out on my shins as it squished shut. I reluctantly turned toward Barry.

"Are you serious?" I asked, hoping it wasn't true and that I misheard him.

He nodded yes.

My breath came back as a labored exhale as I crumpled into a pile on the floor. The light blue linoleum was cold on my bare legs, sending a chill through my entire body and taking my breath away again once more.

I looked up at Barry, my eyes wide with disbelief. I couldn't find words; I was choking on the tears that were threatening to erupt from my eyes.

While I was in a pile on the floor, Jezebel started licking my face and hopping all over me. Barry knew I wasn't getting up anytime soon and sat on the floor with me and held me. The second his arms were around me; all of my defenses came down and I started wailing, sobbing heavily, gasping for breath. Soon enough, both of us were crying.

As I sat there shaking on the floor in Barry's arms, my life with Chris flashed before my eyes.

The summer of 2013 was when we met Chris. I was working at a skydiving center running events, PR, and marketing, while also a member of a competitive skydiving team. Barry was running the skydiving school and was in charge of the Accelerated Freefall Program (AFF), a training progression that leads to earning your United States Parachute Association (USPA) A-License, which allows you to jump by yourself, without being attached to an instructor.

It was a typical high-desert summer day - I had locked myself in my office, trying to get ahead of today's mission: to stay cool as the temperatures climbed above 100 degrees. When three surfers bumbled into the office at the skydiving center ready to start the student training progression, it was a storm of good energy. They came in cracking jokes, complimenting the young women who worked in the office, and their laughter was infectious. I peeked out of my office to assess the shenanigans that were evolving at the customer service desk.

Craig seemed to be the more serious one of the three, but that wasn't saying much. He was average height, stocky build, had a deep tan and salt and pepper hair. The deep tan could be attributed to his work as a boat captain, and when he wasn't doing that, he was body surfing at the Wedge, an iconic surf spot in Newport Beach.

John, who insisted we called him Potato, was a rabble-rouser. Clearly the class clown for all of his life, Potato had an easy demeanor about him. He had a farm - pistachios and lavender - and when it wasn't harvesting time, he was also surfing the Wedge, and now, jumping out of planes.

Finally, Chris. Early 40's, slender build, kind eyes and a smile that would lift the energy of any person, place, or animal in his proximity. Chris was an Army veteran - an intelligence officer - who spoke several different languages and had traveled around the world, including multiple tours through Iran and Iraq, before receiving an honorable discharge in July 2013. He had just gotten home when he, Craig, and Potato surfed into our lives and onto the drop zone. Chris earned his jump wings in the Army but had to go through the progression to earn his civilian skydiving license.

Barry taught them how to skydive that summer, and we were all fast friends. I was training for the USPA National Skydiving Competition with my team that year, and when the guys got their licenses, they told me that they were also starting a skydiving team - Blue Skies and Tube Rides, a nod to their surfing roots and newfound love for the sky - and asked me to be their coach. It was more of an honorary title than anything else, and the guys started calling me Coach. They also started calling Barry "Chandler", a character from North Shore - a cult-classic surfing movie. Chandler was the ever-patient, incredibly wise "Soul Surfer" who surfed for the love of it, not for the fame. We were no longer Sydney and Barry; we were Coach and Chandler.

After a summer full of jumping out of planes, Barry and I visited Chris in Newport Beach with plans to explore the area, have some drinks, and stay the night. We rode bikes around Balboa Island, and the three musketeers showed us all of their favorite spots. We ended up at Cassidy's, a local watering hole where they spent a lot of their time in the summer.

"Their grilled cheese is out of this world," Chris told me when we sidled up to the bar.

After he ordered his food, I followed suit and ordered a grilled cheese with bacon and avocado. When our food arrived, Chris peeled off the top piece of bread and smothered it in Pepper Plant Original Hot Sauce, I did the same, committing myself to a lifetime of needing this sauce on everything I ate from that point forward. The conversation was easy, talking about everything and nothing at all, sharing stories of our travels, chowing down on grilled cheese and rum drinks.

Chris made me feel seen. When he asked questions, he wanted to know what you had to say, and he listened to understand, not to calculate a response. I was drawn to his energy like a moth to a flame. Anyone who could make me laugh as hard and as often as Chris made me laugh was okay in my book. The five of us had been friends for only a few months at that point, but I knew in my heart that we had been friends for lifetimes before this. Sometimes you meet people and you're like *"ooh, I found you!"* - that was how Barry and I felt about these fellas.

After finishing our sandwiches, we piled into the photo booth like a bunch of teenagers and struck some silly poses before returning to our bikes for the ride back to Chris's condo. Despite having a few too many cocktails, we made it home safe and sound, and I was out like a light the second my head hit the pillow.

I woke up in the middle of the night to Barry tapping me on the shoulder, rousing me from drunken slumber, with blood running down the side of his head.

"What happened?" I started screaming and crying.

"Chris and I went out for a nightcap after you fell asleep. We were crossing the street and I got hit by a car."

They were in a crosswalk, walking their bikes across the street a few blocks from the condo. A drunk driver ran a red light and clipped Barry, sending him and the bike onto the hood of the car, rolling onto the windshield and over the back of the vehicle. By some miracle, the gash on his head and a rolled ankle were his only injuries, so he declined an ambulance ride to the hospital. I lost it. I was angry that they went out after I fell asleep, terrified about the sight in front of me, and thankful that it wasn't worse, because my phone was on silent and charging on the other side of the room. If they needed to call me, I wouldn't have known. I was dead to the world when they rolled in. My mind started racing, envisioning the worst-case scenarios.

I'll never forget the look in Chris's eyes. He was scared, apologizing profusely, and felt responsible. It was his idea to go back out.

Coming back to the cold linoleum floor as my little mind-movie came to an end, it broke my heart that one of my most vibrant memories of Chris was him looking so terrified.

The rest of that morning was a blur. Barry peeled me off the floor and we drove to the drop zone in a daze, listening to Ministry's cover of "What a Wonderful World." I cried all the way to work and by the time I walked into the office, my face was red, swollen, and I was having a hard time breathing through my stuffy nose. I walked past my boss, who was also my mentor in the sport, my skydiving coach, a member of my skydiving team, and a personal friend of mine and Barry's. He asked me what was wrong.

"Chris killed himself last night," I said through tears, still shocked by the words as they crossed my lips. Now it was real.

"Why are you so upset? It's not like you knew him for very long. Suicide is selfish, anyway," he said, turning on a dime, leaving me in a puddle of my own tears.

I was a ball of fury, rage, denial, pain, and grief.

January 18, 2014 was the day Chris took his own life, and I had no idea what kind of battle he had been facing. The Chris I knew made me laugh so hard I cried, connected with total strangers the way I always had, and cared deeply about the people in his life. He was one of the brightest lights in our lives at the time, and the fact that he took his own life had me perplexed. How was this possible?

I was searching for answers, stories about Chris, anything that could help me wrap my head around why this brilliant, beautiful man would even consider suicide, let alone follow through. I connected with an old friend of his, Anthony, who wrote a beautiful story for OC Weekly and Maui Time about Chris's life and his passing.

In reading the story that Anthony shared, I learned that Chris applied for mental health benefits with the VA in mid-September after he was discharged, and the process was brutal. He was going to the VA often, sometimes multiple times per week trying to get help. The VA doctors prescribed him the antidepressants Citalopram and Trazodone. In late December, an acupuncturist helped connect some of the dots between what was happening in his mind and body, and told him he had fibromyalgia, brought on by PTSD. He had been having violent nightmares, and in January he started undergoing sleep tests.

Before his death, Chris decided to file for disability with the VA for PTSD. If accepted, they would pay for his medical care for the rest of his life. The filing process required that he outlined every excruciating detail of every event that may have contributed to his PTSD while he was serving.

Just two days after filling out those forms, Chris killed himself.

January 19, 2014, the day after Chris ended his life, was the first domino to fall, sending me on a spiral of trauma, loss, and a seemingly never-ending grief cycle.

Chris's memorial was scheduled to take place during a training camp with my skydiving team. We had a new teammate this year, a woman traveling from Oregon to train with us. I told the team that I wanted to go to Chris's memorial, but my coach insisted I had a commitment to the team and reminded me that my teammate had already booked travel for this training camp.

I chose to train instead of going to his memorial. I regret that choice every day.

At 10:00 a.m., when Chris's memorial paddle-out was scheduled to start at the Wedge in Newport Beach, I was in a Cessna Caravan, climbing to jumping altitude, some 12,000 feet above the ground. My wrist-mounted altimeter had a watch function on it, and I stared at it from the second we got on the plane until the second it turned from 9:59 to 10:00 a.m. My coach told me to focus, to concentrate on the skydive, to prepare for the jump we were about to do. I ignored him and looked at the clock. If I wasn't at the memorial, I wasn't going to miss the moment of silence. Instead of visualizing my skydive, I visualized being part of the paddle-out.

I imagined Chris carving through huge waves with nothing but his body. I saw him laughing, sharing stories, gesticulating wildly.

I landed from that skydive and ran to check my phone. Barry was at the memorial and said he'd be sending pictures and tell me every single detail so I could feel like I was there. He sent a few texts with pictures of the paddle out, and a few videos, showing me how nearly 100 surfers were kicking and paddling and splashing in the water to honor their fallen friend.

My coach came into the room and asked what I was doing. I rushed to hide my phone like a scared little girl and ran out to the bathroom to cry. When I sat down on the toilet, I screamed silently into my arm, tears freefalling from my face. I swore to myself at that moment that if I ever had to choose between the team and my friends ever again, that I would choose my friends, without question.

On May 9, 2014, I got a call from my dad. My Uncle Mike had passed away peacefully in his sleep. In the years leading up to his death, however, his life was anything but peaceful. My uncle was a gay man, born and raised in Kansas City in the '50s and '60s. He was a singer, actor, entrepreneur, designer, and creator. He was the personification of love. By the time I was old enough to understand who he was to me, he was splitting his time between New York and San Francisco. He had found two amazing communities on the coasts that were much more welcoming than where he grew up in Kansas.

One of my most vivid memories with my uncle was when he showed me pictures from Burning Man. He and his creative cohorts had a camp there for years, and when he showed me photos from one of his art installations, I thought it was fake. There was no way there was this much art, these many people dressed in so many creative costumes, surrounded by this blank canvas of desert dust. Growing up in the suburbs of Kansas City, I hadn't seen deserts before. I didn't know that Burning Man was real, I just thought my uncle liked dressing up and digitally manipulating pictures.

After I moved to Southern California in 2011, my uncle was diagnosed with brain cancer. He had an inoperable glioblastoma, and they gave him a couple of years to live, tops. He beat brain cancer the first time, and when I saw him at my grandmother's funeral in 2012, I was old enough to understand what that meant. I knew I was standing in the presence of a medical miracle. The therapies they had done and the tumor itself had impacted his speaking and singing voice, and it was heartbreaking to hear him try to find the words that had so effortlessly floated from his lips for decades prior. Even though his voice wasn't what it once was, it was still beautiful.

I found out that his memorial would be happening at my cousin's house in Kansas, so I asked my family what their plans were. They couldn't afford to go so they weren't planning to attend. All of my money was going to rent, student loans, food, insurance, and team training. I didn't want to go without my family, so I passed on the opportunity to celebrate my uncle's life.

The weekend before my uncle's memorial, one of my teammates injured herself on a training jump. We didn't think she would heal in time, so we didn't seek a replacement flyer to train with for the National Skydiving Championships later that year. It rocked my world because we were on fire. Our training so far had been going really well and it looked like we could potentially earn a medal at Nationals. I had invested so much time, energy, and money into this team and into developing my individual skills, that when an injury effectively rendered our season over, I was crushed.

I was also secretly relieved because, after my coach's comment about Chris, my patience with him was wearing thin. We ceased our training and I had to reckon with my own demons: was skydiving worth the risk?

Was team training worth the investment? I was pissed at my teammate for getting injured. I couldn't even look at her. It was a dumb mistake on her part, one that could most definitely have been avoided, and I was still reeling from losing Chris and my uncle. On top of that, I was furious because I had skipped my Uncle Mike's memorial because I didn't have the money. If I had known that she was going to get injured and that I wouldn't be paying for training later that month, I could have gone. Of course, that's not something I could have predicted, but I berated myself for years for not knowing better.

Aside from my marriage, skydiving was one of the only areas of my life that felt like it was going right, that I could count on, that I could pour myself into. Now that rug had been ripped out from under me. I'm a silver-lining kind of gal, so once I got over my petty temper tantrum, I held on to hope that she would recover in time for us to compete. We had worked so hard and were having so much fun, I still wanted to see that through.

On August 2, 2014, I woke up ahead of my alarm and started scrolling mindlessly through Facebook. I saw my friend Eric had changed his Facebook picture to be a photo of him and my friend Adam. Another friend posted a photo on Adam's wall. All of the hair stood up on the back of my neck and I started to panic. There was a strange phenomenon in the skydiving community that when people died; everyone changed their Facebook profile photo to a black square to indicate that someone close to them had died. This wasn't a black square but considering that Adam was in Idaho on a BASE-jumping trip, it felt like I got socked in the stomach and my anxious brain started to assume the worst. It was early in the morning, but I sent Adam a message at 5:57 a.m., hoping he'd respond and put my worries to rest:

How is everything going? Miss your face!
Nationals here we come!

Then I scrolled up to see our previous messages to each other.

July 22, 2014 - 11:01 p.m. - ADAM

What's up miss how's the chalet and
dogs doing :)

July 23, 2014 - 9:21 a.m. - ME

They be good. How are you? Busy jumping off stuff?

July 23, 2014 - 12:58 p.m. - ADAM

Yup pretty much. I got offered a job to
help tom a's first jump course packing
and helping the other coaches in the
school. I'll be getting flown to Idaho
5-10 times a year and in return learn a
ton about rigging and staying alive in
the sport.

I didn't respond to that message. I was probably busy at work and forgot. But the part about staying alive in the sport made me feel like I was going to vomit.

Our most recent messages were from July 28. He was asking about how many jumps he could make in a day, because he needed to do a certain amount of jumps in a specific time window and was trying to figure out where he could get the most jumps in, at the skydiving center where I worked or somewhere else. I had responded but I was short, I didn't ask him what the goal was, I just gave him the answer he was looking for.

It was a Saturday morning and we opened early on the weekends, so I got in the shower and started getting my stuff together for a day on the drop zone.

In the shower, I started to feel really sick and I needed answers. When I got out, I sent Eric a message at 6:51a.m.:

> I hate that I'm asking this because it's fucking ridiculous how Facebook has washed my brain, but is Adam okay? Saw your pic with him and Dojo posted to his wall and hoping it's just a lot of love for how awesome Adam is, but worried that he's hurt or something. Know he's up at the bridge and busy jumping off stuff so just being a concerned "Barry taught him how to skydive so he's kind of like my kid or brother" kind of lady.

Adam, like Chris, was another one of Barry's Kidz - our nickname for the folks who learned how to skydive under Barry's supervision. Adam learned how to skydive in eight days. This was a miracle mostly because of how finicky the Illinois weather can be in the summer. It's very rare to get eight jumpable days in a row between thunderstorms, potential tornado activity, and high winds. But Adam had the perfect window and earned his A-License in just eight days. When we moved from Chicago to Southern California in late 2011, Adam wasn't far behind. He came to visit and then he eventually moved to California as well. He lived with us for a bit in 2012 and was Jezebel's favorite new human in the house.

That morning, like the moments after Barry told me that Chris had killed himself, everything was moving in slow motion. Our friends Tom and Tracy, two of my competitive mentors, had recently moved out to SoCal. They were also from the drop zone in Illinois, and we had a nice little contingent of Chicago skydivers slowly infiltrating this drop zone. They were at the skydiving center that morning, and I sat outside chatting with Tom for a bit, venting my frustrations with not being able to train and talking about how much I missed doing team jumps since my teammate was injured.

I went back into my office to check my email and post on Facebook to get more people to come out and jump over the weekend when my phone rang. It was Eric.

"Is Adam okay?" I asked, praying it was a yes, but feeling deep in my soul that it was a no.

I don't remember exactly what Eric said, but I ran out of that office wailing. Adam was dead.

Later conversations would reveal that he had been helping with first jump courses, as he said he would be in his earlier messages to me. They had decided to jump somewhere that Adam hadn't jumped before, a cliff. He had been doing bridge jumps with no problems, but on this particular jump, his canopy opened off-heading, turning him away from his desired flight path and toward the cliff. He struck the cliff he jumped off of, falling some 200-feet after the initial impact. One of the people he was jumping with administered CPR while they waited for the medics. He died before the medics could save him.

Everything else was a blur, and my memory of what happened next is spotty, but I remember running out of the office, grabbing Barry as well as Tom and Tracy. I don't remember if I was able to get them into a team room to break the news or if I told them right then and there, but all I knew was Adam was dead, and these people needed to know.

I tried to work that day. I tried to do anything other than cry. Eventually, my coach made his way to the drop zone. He asked Barry what happened, and Barry told him.

"Well that's a choice he made, to jump off the cliff," he said callously.

Shortly after speaking with Barry, my coach found me to let me know that my teammate made a full recovery and the team wanted to resume training and go to Nationals.

No acknowledgment of the fact that someone who I considered a little brother had just died. No consideration for my feelings. Just an insult about BASE jumping to my husband and the only thing he said to me was letting me know that the team wanted to go to Nationals after all.

I took the rest of the day off, went to the liquor store, and got all the supplies for our community that was grieving - tons and tons of beer. I was waiting to hear about memorial services and needed to figure out how we were going to get to Illinois. I looked at my bank account.

I only had enough money to get us to Nationals OR Adam's funeral. Both would be happening in Illinois, and we couldn't afford to take two trips. I had a choice to make, and after skipping the memorials for Chris and my uncle, I knew what I was going to do.

When I got home from Adam's funeral in Illinois, it was time to jump into preparations for the biggest event of the year at the drop zone. The timing was perfect, actually, because this was one thing I could throw myself into. And did I ever. As the event neared, I pulled all of the tricks out of my marketing hat and made sure that it was the biggest, best, most well-attended event that drop zone had ever seen.

And it was.

A few days later, I woke up to a text message from a friend. It was a screenshot of a Facebook comment accusing my coach of raping a 14-year-old girl. I lost it. I wanted to throw up. I went straight into detective mode and hopped on the county court website to see if I could find the arrest records.

Still lying in bed, scrolling through arrest records on my phone, I found his record. My stomach sank down to my toes as I read the words on the screen. Six felony charges. As I read, my vision started crossing and I felt like I was going to throw up. Preventing the victim from reporting. Unlawful sex with a minor. Lewd and lascivious acts with a minor under 14, with force. Oral copulation with a person under 16. Penetration with a person under 18.

I passed my phone to Barry.

Things started to make sense. Between the comments about Chris and Adam, the flip-flopping on whether or not we were going to Nationals, and my choice to go to Adam's funeral over competing with my team, my relationship with my coach had been deteriorating and we were barely speaking to each other. He was short with me, and I just wanted to do my job. I took a break from jumping when Adam died, and he wasn't happy about it. When I started working for him, he clearly stated that he wanted me to be jumping all the time with as many people as possible. He was upset with me for not jumping during this period of time, as if my grief were an inconvenience to his personal and professional life. As a result, I was questioning how long it was taking me to grieve – should I be ready to jump by now? *Was* I overreacting?

He hadn't been on the drop zone since the big event, and now it made sense. He was arrested a few days after the event ended and was laying low. Barry and I decided to say nothing and see how it played out.

Within a few days, word started to get out. Other people saw the Facebook comments and did their own digging. Barry and I were at an event in San Diego when we got a call from an instructor, asking what we knew. We told them what we found, and the arrest records indicated that he had a court date coming up. The next day we went back to the drop zone and I spoke with his business partner.

At the time I was the director of events, marketing, and public relations for this business, and a fully sponsored competitive skydiver. With one of the owners being arrested on six felony counts of various degrees of sexual assault with a minor, I did not want this to be my responsibility to clean up if it blew back on the business. If this was true, and I had a feeling it was, I could not continue to do my job, generating revenue for the business, and lining the pockets of a sexual predator. This was not how my legacy in this sport was going to play out.

My coach's business partner defended him in that meeting. He said that the victim was making it up, and she was starved for attention. After the meeting, my coach walked around telling everyone that we shouldn't worry – what happened was consensual.

The stories weren't lining up and I knew this was going to get messy.

I turned in my resignation that day. I gave them until the end of the year, said I'd help find and train my replacement, and offered to write out a manual for whoever stepped in to replace me. The work I did affected every area of the business; new tandem students, skydiving students going through the training program, keeping the student engaged and in the community after graduation, and making this drop zone the best place in the world to jump out of planes for experienced skydivers. My job was multifaceted and when done correctly, was a major revenue driver for the business.

My last skydive was on my last day at work, December 29, 2014.

CHAPTER 2

GIRL, HOW DID
WE GET HERE?

2015 was a wild ride as well. After leaving my dream job and walking away from my sponsorships and ambitious goal of being a World Champion Skydiver, I had some unfinished business in the sport and wanted to prove that I could do this by myself without a big drop zone behind me. I wanted to know - was I really good at events or was I riding the coattails of a sexual predator and a prestigious skydiving center? Could I sell-out events that I created by myself? What kind of events would I want to go to if I was still interested in jumping out of planes?

I created a skydiving events company called Planet Green Socks, named after the green socks that Adam wore on his skydives and BASE jumps, and a nod to our shared desire to travel around the world. I created skills camps for experienced skydivers in Southern California and brought in some of the best athletes in the sport to lead the camps. Every event we created sold out and everyone had an incredible time. But I was still unhappy. It didn't matter if I was doing events on my own or for a big skydiving center, this wasn't my passion anymore. Between all the deaths, my competitive career being dependent on the condition of a teammate's knee, and my coach being charged with these felonies, the love was lost. The risk wasn't worth the reward for me on jumping, I knew that much. And the financial risk I was taking to host these events wasn't worth it for me either.

The last event I hosted in skydiving was Adam's memorial event. It occurred in May 2015, eight months after Adam died. It was an incredibly emotional experience, and as his fellow teammates and friends released his ashes into the sky, I knew my time in the sport was over. I wouldn't say it was the perfect way to end my time in skydiving, but it felt like a nice bow on a beautiful, if not tragic, chapter of my life.

A few months after Adam's memorial, Barry lost his job and his dream. He had been a professional skydiver for 16 years at that point and it ended in a proverbial dumpster fire with one of the owners. There was a lot of drama in the aftermath of my old coach being convicted on two of the six felony counts, and my husband got caught in the crosshairs. When they didn't replace me after my departure, marketing effectively stopped on my last day, and the business started to suffer. My husband was let go because the student retention numbers were down. Not by any fault of his own, as his responsibility was to safely train and retain the students that came through the door, not new student acquisition. When you stop marketing your business and your reputation is tarnished, people aren't going to spend their money there and they will train elsewhere. The drop zone we'd worked at was the pinnacle of student skydiving operations, and to go anywhere else would have been a significant step backward.

The months that followed were brutal, and we both started drinking heavily. I was looking for answers to life's problems in the bottom of a bottle of a wine bottle or a pint of Ben & Jerry's, and I was eating everything in sight.

After Barry lost his job, we needed to get away. We decided to take a road trip around California with our dogs, camping in Joshua Tree, Stanislaus National Forest, Limekiln State Park, and a host of other areas between San Diego and the Bay Area. I fell in love with the redwood trees and envisioned a life of adventure in the outdoors.

In October, we drove up to Portland, Oregon to see some friends. On the way back home to SoCal from the trip, as we were driving past Mount Shasta, I was on the phone with my mentor who was working at the agency I left when I decided to skydive full-time. I asked if there were any opportunities at the agency. I shared that I retired from skydiving entirely and took some time to myself to figure out what I wanted. I wanted stability. A good paycheck and benefits package. A smart team to work with. Big clients. I wanted to be back in agency land, I wanted to feel useful and professional and confident in my skills again.

In late 2015, I ended up going back to the agency as a contractor. Jumping back into corporate work felt incredible. The pace was fast, and I was refreshed, ready to take on everything that could possibly come my way.

When we moved to San Diego the following year, it was a clean slate. I paid off my debt from when I was training with my skydiving team and started making a bigger dent in my student loans. We had enough money to do whatever we wanted, within reason. I wasn't going to be buying a boat or a plane or anything but compared to the measly wage I was being paid while I worked in skydiving, I was finally able to relax and breathe a little. We replaced our donated furniture. We got a new bed. I filled the house in San Diego with things I'd always wanted - a Vitamix, a KitchenAid mixer, the perfect grey couch, a standing desk for my home office, and a gorgeous little oasis in the backyard.

Everything was easy. And the ease made me nervous. After so many years of things being decidedly difficult, ease felt hard to trust.

My parents were stoked that I wasn't jumping out of planes anymore. I had a big paycheck, cushy benefits, and I was launching a new wine brand and working with Fortune 500 companies like Intel, Comcast, and NBC Universal - household names that made for good bragging rights. Everything in my life looked like it was turning around. I was adulting.

The agency I was working with ceased operations entirely from Christmas through New Year's, so Barry and I were looking for something to do during the break. Donald Trump had just been elected President of the United States, I was feeling fire and fury for all of the issues that were springing up around that, and I just needed to get away. I thought back to the road trip we had taken the year before, about the redwoods, about how comfortable I felt in a tent. I wanted to spend some time outside.

At the time, there were pipeline protests happening up at Standing Rock. We felt called to go help out and started to make arrangements. The tribe had been posting about welcoming new volunteers to help protest the building of the pipeline, listing supplies they needed, and giving regular updates about what was happening on the reservation.

At the beginning of December, we had a quick weekend campout in Joshua Tree with some friends. I had fallen in love with the desert and needed to clear my head. After two nights in the wilderness with no cell reception, away from all the news and notifications, I felt a bit more human. When we got home, the folks at Standing Rock were asking anyone who was planning on coming to please stay home. They had an abundance of boots on the ground and the weather was starting to turn.

So, we turned to the trusty internet. Given how much I liked camping and day hikes, Barry asked if I wanted to go on a backpacking trip. I was nervous but excited. I remembered Adam telling me about his desire to hike the Pacific Crest Trail and started getting excited about doing a shorter version of a long-distance hike.

We were looking for something that we could do in a week, a good entry-level distance for someone who hasn't done more than one day of hiking in a row. And if it was local to Southern California, even better.

A few Google searches later, we found the Trans-Catalina Trail. This was a point-to-point hike, 38.5 miles across Catalina Island, right off the coast of Los Angeles. We watched some YouTube videos and read some blog posts of folks who had completed this thru-hike and we were enamored by the ocean views, remote backcountry, and beach campsites.

We booked the trip and started making a list of gear that I needed to get, as I had never been backpacking before. After doing a bunch of research, we had a great starter list. I wanted to go somewhere I could try everything on, see how it fit and feel confident in what I'm purchasing before I invest a significant amount of money into this equipment.

And with that, we made our way to a store that sold outdoor equipment.

Once inside the store, I made my way to the hiking apparel section. I found a shirt and a pair of pants I liked, grabbed the sizes I usually wear, and scurried off to the dressing room.

"HIKING! We're doing this!" I thought to myself.

I yanked my pants down, tore off my shirt.

"I'm going to hike across Catalina Island!"

I took the pants off the hanger and slid the moisture-wicking fabric over my right leg.

"Oooh, these are niiiice," I thought as I pulled on the other pant leg.

Uh oh. I couldn't pull the pants all the way up, and there was exactly zero percent chance that I'd be able to button them if I did.

Maybe outdoor gear is sized differently.

I took off the tight pants and put my own pants back on. As I was pulling up my flowy pants with an elastic waistband, I had a flashback to the first time I remember caring about sizes on clothes: my freshman year of high school, trying on cheerleading uniforms.

It was so vivid that I felt like I was time traveling and was actually my freshman-year self, back in the locker room, trying on my uniform.

As I walked through the halls after school, making my way to cheerleading practice, I was so excited. Today was uniform fitting day. I did it. After years of cheering for Pop Warner Football, taking gymnastics classes, and practicing very hard, I was a high school cheerleader. One of the reasons I was so excited was simply the uniform itself. The high school uniforms had sparkly metallic gold accents instead of the mustard yellow accents that we had on our uniforms when we cheered for Pop Warner Football as kids. Now we were bright and shiny and sparkly. Our poms had gold metallic in them too. No more of that trash-bag material, these were REAL poms.

The uniform fitting days were set up like an assembly line with all of the uniform components stacked in piles by size. The first size I tried was too small. There was an eyeroll and exasperation in the coach's facial expression when I came back for a bigger size. I remember her handing me a size 9 skirt, and I started comparing. The other girls were wearing smaller sizes, much smaller. My world wasn't shattered, I didn't have some Hollywood-worthy meltdown, but standing in front of the mirror in my size 9 skirt, I pulled my signature "get smaller" move. I stood up on my tiptoes and sucked in, holding my breath, seeing what I would look like if

I were thinner. Like many moments over the course of my life, I saw my thinner body and longed to appear smaller. I locked in my mission: get a "hot" body. Be smaller.

I snapped back to the dressing room, standing there staring at myself, 32 years old.

I sheepishly hung up the pants that wouldn't fit and went back out to the rack. I looked at the largest size they had, a 16. Knowing I couldn't even get the 12s over my hips, I reluctantly grabbed the 16s, passing over size 14, each size tag screaming at me like a judgment: *"Keep moving, fatty, and don't collect $200."*

The enthusiasm that had me inflated, light, floating around the Encinitas REI store was now seeping out of my body, leaking like air out of a balloon. I pulled the door closed behind me and took a deep breath.

I held my breath as I shimmied into the bigger size. They were tighter than I thought they would be, and this was the largest size available. No other brands here make pants bigger than these. I wanted hiking pants, not some knockoff brand or poorly made pair of pants from a store that sells bigger sizes. As I sat down, the waistband dug into my mid-section. I stood up, looked at the length of the pants and shook my head. Apparently, all women who are a size 16 are also professional basketball players, because these pants were too long. I stood up on my tippy toes and sucked in. I started to wonder if this dressing room is actually a time machine because I was thrust back into another flashback, this time, a conversation with my mom.

When I was younger, my mom said to me, "Sydney, you'd better watch what you eat, because if you don't, you'll end up like me."

I was young and didn't understand. *What does she mean? I'll end up being a cool cheer mom? I'll give the shirt off my back for someone in need? Why is that bad and what does that have to do with the food I eat?*

My mother is fat and has been since she had babies and stopped smoking cigarettes As a family, we were always trying some new diet: Atkins, Weight Watchers, low-fat everything. I observed how my mom looked at herself in the mirror, how she spoke about her body. It was never explicitly taught or said, but my young mind came to understand that in this house, bigger bodies were bad, and smaller bodies were good. As I grew up, media, books, music, movies, and TV shows all confirmed my suspicions.

I know now that my mom meant well when she told me this, but back then, all it did was instill in me a fear of being fat. Even when I was fit and healthy, I felt the need to be smaller, with a body like a Victoria's Secret model and hair like you see in an Herbal Essences commercial.

I didn't ask any follow-up questions. I was a young girl, already addicted to earning gold stars, being THE BEST AND FIRST at everything, and I didn't want my mom to think I was stupid by asking questions, so I nodded and made a note to always watch what I eat so I wouldn't end up fat like my mother.

Back in a body I don't recognize in this dressing room, I slid the XL shirt off the hanger, also the biggest size they carry in this store, and squeezed the buttons together around my belly button. This shirt has buttons that snap, and I didn't know how to feel about that. I imagined a button popping off on-trail, taking out one of Barry's eyes, leaving us stranded, down one eye in the backcountry, because I'm too fat for this shirt. So, I guess it's better that the shirt snaps, so we don't have a traditional button blowout. But then I worried about my shirt just ripping open like tearaway pants, my exposed body sending a shockwave in every direction, wiping out any and all plants, animals, and human beings in its wake.

This is how things go for me. This is how my brain works.

"Prepare for the worst, expect the best," has taught me to always identify and prepare for the absolute worst-case scenario before even considering that something could be normal, or okay, or maybe even terrific.

I snapped out of my shame spiral. After all, everything I've read says this is the style of shirt I want. I don't want cotton for a backpacking trip, I want something that will dry quickly and protect me from the sun.

Feeling a bit like a sausage about to split its casing in this new attire, I paused and looked at myself in the mirror. Typically for me, going shopping includes a lot of self-judgment. I'll pick and poke at the parts of my body that I desperately want to fix while saying unkind things to myself about myself. The train of thought about the button was exhausting. I let out a sigh and started to disrobe when I recalled a meme that said something along the lines of *"if you wouldn't dream of saying it to your best friend, don't say it to yourself."*

I shrugged at myself in the mirror, continuing the conversation I was having in my head. I pretended that I was talking to my best friend in the mirror. She would never be on the receiving end of the terrible things I say to myself, or the scenarios I prepare for. No way, no how. I thought of how I'd start a conversation with my best friend, and we always start with an emphatic *"GIRL."*

"GIRL," I said to myself, leaning all my weight on my left hip, gesturing wildly around this body I didn't recognize, *"how did we get here?"*

It was a rhetorical question for the dressing room, but as I scanned my body head to toe, I started to connect the dots. My hair was the longest it had ever been, I had straightened it stick straight and kept up on my highlights, inching closer and closer to the type of woman I always envisioned I would be - fit, blonde, living near the beach in California. Short of having the perfect body, I checked off some of the success boxes I had achieved thus far: long blonde hair, great job with a great salary, living in SoCal, married to the man of my dreams, and we just moved into the perfect house in San Diego. As I was standing in this dressing room in Encinitas, California, I gave younger me a shout out. Younger me, the girl who grew up in Kansas watching "The OC" and "The Hills", was getting ready for her first backpacking trip. We had been living in Southern California for five years, and the part of me that aspired to be like the girls on "The OC" felt mildly satisfied. *"When I get thin, then I'll have it all."*

I flexed my muscles in the mirror, not because I had any, but because I wanted to stress test this shirt. It was a bit tight, and I didn't want to Hulk out of it on the trail like I did one of my shirts at a concert the year prior. So, I did my best Arnold Schwarzenegger poses and the material was surprisingly forgiving, even a bit stretchy.

I did some squats in the pants, stepped up on the bench to replicate taking big steps up on the trail, making sure I didn't split them open or pop a button. Again, pretty stretchy, pretty forgiving.

My stretching and flexing and stepping had me breathless in the dressing room. I moved closer to the mirror, almost booping my own nose on the glass, staring into my own eyes. I took a deep breath, closed my eyes, and instead of judging myself for working up a sweat trying on clothes, I looked at myself dead in the eyes and half-asked, half-told myself:

"What would be possible if we honored our inner athlete? From here on out, with this hike moving forward, could we try that?"

I nodded at myself in the mirror. I did another scan of my body and didn't judge it, just observed. As I took off the biggest sizes I had ever tried on and slid back into the comfortable clothes I arrived in, I felt a bit lighter. I had a bit more pep to my step after I left that store.

CHAPTER 3

CHICKEN AND DUMPLINGS

Two weeks later, it was showtime. Time to hike across Catalina Island.

One of Barry's former skydiving students offered us a place to crash the night before our hike, so we made our way to Long Beach to catch up. By the time we got there through traffic, we were starving. We checked out their new place, did some casual catching up, and then we took their boat over to Ballast Point for dinner and drinks. As we were cruising through canals and into the bay, I could see Catalina Island. It looked small and huge at the same time. As I looked at the island, I wondered if I would be able to make it across in one piece. I had all the gear now, but we hadn't been training or anything. I just rolled off the couch and onto the trail after two of the hardest years of my life. When we moved to the house in San Diego, I purchased a standing desk, but that was the extent of my physical activity in those days.

After one too many beers, I struggled to fall asleep. I was nervous, excited, and uncertain of what would happen on this trip. I tossed and turned until I finally passed out. I woke up to my alarm, scrambling for my stuff in the dark, strapped on my backpack to take it down to the car, and got in the elevator with Barry. In case we died on the first day, I wanted to get a selfie of us before we even got to the island.

"HERE WE GO!" I posted to Facebook.

We made it to the ferry landing, parked the car, checked in, and sat in the lobby to wait to get in line for our ferry over to Avalon, the beginning of this journey.

The ferry ride was a blur of excitement and nervous energy. I mentally reviewed the items in my backpack, making sure I didn't forget anything. I had all the essentials and a few items that made Barry roll his eyes. (What do you mean "normal people" don't bring a deck of tarot cards on a backpacking trip?)

I was ready.

The first day on the Trans-Catalina Trail is the hardest – you're traveling 11 miles, hiking up and down five peaks, carrying all of your food and water for this adventure. My pack was the heaviest it was ever going to be. As I shouldered it to disembark the ferry, I looked around.

Catalina Island was one of the first places outside of Kansas that I visited when I was a kid. My dad called it a "throwaway" port on the first west coast cruise we took when I was in high school. Now, as I made my way off the ferry and started navigating through Avalon, I racked my brain for memories here. I didn't have any. Did we even get off the ship? I thought at least something would look familiar, nope.

We ventured through town, trying to find the building for the Catalina Island Conservancy, where we would check in. As we turned the corner, I spotted the building shown in the YouTube videos we watched before this hike – white with blue trim. We walked over, checked in, got a map of the island, and began to make our way toward the trailhead. Having taken the 6 a.m. ferry over from Long Beach so we could get started bright and early, this sleepy island town was just starting to rise and shine.

As we walked through Avalon, we got turned around and walked in the opposite direction of the trailhead. When we realized this, we stopped to get our bearings and made our way to Hermit Gulch.

My eyes tell the whole story of this first backpacking trip.

The trail continued out the back of the campground and a series of aggressive switchbacks led us up and out of the canyon. As we gained elevation climbing up to the ridgeline, I could see the cruise ships on the horizon, waiting to pull into port.

In my mind, I heard my dad joking about the "wasted time" on Catalina Island en route to Ensenada, Mexico. *"It's a throwaway day because we just sit out here all night, sailing in circles until it's time to pull into port.*

They should have just taken off at sailaway, floored it over here, and docked last night. But nooooo, we have to wait until the morning and then waste a whole day here."

An hour or two into this adventure, I felt my right shoe rubbing on the outside of my heel, the beginning stages of a blister. Barry described this as a "hot spot" when he was helping me get prepared for this hike, and he advised that if I felt this start to happen, we should stop hiking and handle it, hopefully avoiding a blister altogether.

So, I stopped. I looked around for a level place to put my pack, but I couldn't find one. I had visions of having a Cheryl Strayed moment up here, sending my shoe over the side of the mountain down toward the cruise ships. Never one to miss an opportunity to one-up tragic thoughts, my imagination sent my backpack sailing behind the shoe. On the trail, I positioned my pack against the slope of the mountain this switchback was cut into. Everything was steep. Everything was hurting. I was having a hard time catching my breath during this aggressive climb out of the canyon. Barry handed me the roll of Leukotape and walked me through how to tape up the affected area. It felt better when I put my socks and shoes on, and we continued hiking.

It was December, but it felt like July. While the temperature never rose above 75 degrees, there is no coverage or shade on this trail, only full sun. I was struggling physically, feeling other hot spots develop on both feet. My toes felt cramped and crushed in my shoes. *When will these switchbacks end? Does this trail ever flatten out or is the entire hike going to be an uphill climb, kicking up dust and sending waves of heat rising from the ground?* It felt like I opened the oven door and stuck my face in the blast of hot air. I couldn't help but laugh at myself and my lack of preparation, as evidenced by my blisters. *"Well, apparently wearing hiking boots at your standing desk is not the same as breaking them in, Sydney."*

As we were hiking, Barry would occasionally turn around and shout back to me, "PROUD OF YOU!"

The first time he said it, it made me cry. I didn't know if I could do this. I didn't know if we'd make it to the end in one piece, but I knew I wanted to try. As we came over the crest to the first rest area on this section of trail, I was so relieved. The shade structure didn't offer much by means of shade, but it was nice to take my pack off. I did a scan of my body, hyper-aware of every ache and pain. I was parched and sucked down water while taking in the scenery around me. As I took some deep breaths to try to slow my heart rate, I noticed the air smelled sweeter at this elevation.

In the distance to the east, I could see the mainland – downtown Long Beach, piers up and down the coast, boats sailing in and out of the port. I could see a cruise ship tender boat bringing folks to Avalon. I could see how far we had come since we started and while I had already earned my title as mayor of blister town, I was starting to understand why Barry likes doing this so much.

Barry grew up in New Hampshire and has hiked most of the White Mountains and Presidential range, most of which with his dog. When I moved to Austin in the fall after we met, Barry did a walkabout in Texas, covering 100-something miles in less than a week. He had always told me that hiking was exercise that didn't feel like exercise and that the fresh air and views always made up for how hard it may be to get to the top of some of these places or to cover longer distances.

The first hike I remember doing with Barry was remarkably similar to this moment on the trail, except I was in way better shape. Before we moved to California, I had been running every day, so the transition to hiking felt natural and easy. Our first hike together was somewhere in the Ortega Mountains near our house in Lake Elsinore, California. Barry had promised me we could go visit Stone Brewing Company and grab some food when we finished the hike. As we were making our way through the high desert terrain - dusty, hot, exposed - I kept asking how much further. He kept shouting back to me, "just around the bend!"

For hours and hours, he kept telling me were almost there. I was frustrated beyond belief, desperate to arrive at these views he kept insisting were worth the pain I was in - as I didn't break those shoes in, either. I bought them at the Merrell Outlet the day before and figured I'd be good to go for a 12-mile jaunt through the wilderness. When we finally made it to the top on that first hike, I surrendered to the moment - he was right. The views *were* worth the effort. Afterward, I felt incredibly accomplished sitting in the corner booth at Stone, devouring duck confit tacos like someone was going to take them away from me. I didn't understand the power of hiker hunger back then, but I did develop a hunger for hiking, and I was ravenous for more.

Over the course of the next five years, we were fair-weather hikers. Fair weather doesn't reflect our level of stoke on hiking, we just prefer to hike in fair weather. Living in the high desert limited our hiking season to late fall and winter. In 2015, on a road trip around California, we car camped and did short hikes with the dogs. That's when I started to seriously consider what it would take to do the Pacific Crest Trail or another long scenic trail.

When we found the Trans-Catalina Trail, I thought it could be a good warmup to see if I could handle thru-hiking. The Trans-Catalina Trail covers 38.5 miles of Santa Catalina Island, and while it's remote, yes, you're never days away from getting help like you are on the longer trails. And while we need to carry all of our food for this journey, every campground has water – the first three campgrounds have running water, and the last one, Parsons Landing, has water delivered to you in a locker since there isn't running water available. It takes the scary part away and leaves you with some pretty basic things to evaluate: do I like being out here for days on end? Can I sleep well on the trail? How does my body respond to days in a row of longer hikes? If I enjoy it, and I can physically handle it, then the hard stuff is worth the sacrifice.

So far, the hike had been pretty brutal. In the videos we watched from other folks who have done this trail, we noticed that there was a playground in the middle of the backcountry, and they were saying it was about the half-way point for the first day. I looked at the map as we started to pack up to keep going, evaluating how my body felt. We were at mile three at this first shade structure and I already had blisters forming. The playground was near mile six, and our first campground was between mile 10 and 11. Even though we got a bit turned around at the beginning, I was thankful we didn't take the route that loops around the Wrigley property. If we had gone that route, we would have added four miles to the journey. Who knows what kind of condition I would have been in?

In the heart of the backcountry on Santa Catalina Island.

As we made our way further into the interior of the island, Barry and I noticed the landscape had shifted a bit. We alternated between fire roads and single-track, sometimes with 360-degree ocean views. Even though my feet were killing me, it was so beautiful that it was almost enough to make me forget about the pain. We reached a place that is perfect for photos, with a water view, and I raised my hands in the air for the first full-body photo I had taken in a long time. I wanted some sweet outdoor goddess photos to share on Instagram, to document this journey. As we left this spot, we started to descend into a canyon, and I was thankful for the break from climbing.

I started daydreaming about what the next day would bring as we walked past fields of sage plants, each step a welcome respite for my aching legs. The next section from Blackjack Campground to Little Harbor was primarily downhill after we passed the Airport in the Sky. Downhill felt so good after miles of uphill climbing to get to the ridge line. I imagined the most luxurious cruise into our second campground, and an even more relaxing day off in Little Harbor the day after. As I lifted my head out of my daydream, I see the playground. They weren't kidding, it's a full-on playground in the middle of the backcountry.

As we came up closer to the playground, I started thinking of ways I could extend our break here and delay our return to the trail. I was in the most pain I had ever been in recent memory and I couldn't stop sweating. I knew Barry would love me regardless of my performance on this trip, but I didn't want to leave anything to chance. I really wanted to be good at this. At this point we were six miles in, and I hadn't done anything longer than this since we first moved to California five years prior. As we roll up on the playground, I start to execute phase one of my procrastination strategy - bust out the GoPro to get some footage of me swinging on the swings. My intention was two-fold: delay as much as possible while trying to "get the shot" and move as much air across my sweaty body as possible. It was just me and Barry at this playground, nobody else. I took off my pack, enjoying the release as the weight comes off of my shoulders.

After ample shots of me on the swings, pointing out plants and animals, and doing everything I can to give my legs a break, Barry started tapping his wrist.

"If we want to get to this campground before sunset, we need to get moving. We don't want to be out here in the dark with bison on-trail."

As we packed up, I was inspired by how far we had already come, and I was thoroughly looking forward to something other than jerky to eat. I wanted a *meal*. Something with substance. While we were making our way up and down more peaks, I feel my right hip flexor start to get aggravated. I remembered hearing in a yoga class that a lot of trauma and memories are stored in our hips, and as I relived one of the most soul-crushing moments of my life, I felt like I understood what that yoga teacher meant.

As I was hiking through the pain, I heard a voice in my head. It was my rowing coach from the University of Kansas,

"Drive backward with your ass, Sydney."

I was on the erg, an indoor rowing machine, doing sprints with the team after an early morning weight training session. The mission of this particular drill was to get our split times as low as possible. No matter how hard I tried, I couldn't get my time down. We focused on my body position and it clicked for my coach - I wasn't driving with my legs, I was just going through the motions. My form was great, but I wasn't adding power.

I pushed off the balls of my feet, driving back with my butt as I extended my legs, and I felt a pang of pain. I slowed down to a stop and signaled for my coach. Something wasn't right. I made my way down to the athletic trainer and sat down on the table for an evaluation. The trainer moved my leg in all different directions, keeping the pressure on my hip flexor area as he manipulated my body position.

"You have a severe strain of your hip flexor; you're going to need to come see me before and after every practice until we get this sorted out."

I spent most of the spring season on the bench waiting for my hip to heal. For most of my life leading up to my time on the rowing team at KU, I was a cheerleader, so I brought my enthusiasm to practice every day. After getting to the training facility early to try a variety of stretches and electronic stimulation, I'd cheer on my teammates during their runs, during their drills, and as they brought the boats back after training on the water. It was heartbreaking to watch my teammates train and compete without me, but what was I supposed to do? I kept a smile on my face, hoping my enthusiasm would buy me some time to recover and show that I could do this.

I made plans to live with my teammates at Jayhawk Towers - housing specifically for student-athletes across the street from the training center. I made plans to row Varsity and swore I would do anything I needed to do to get up to speed after my hip healed.

When the spring season wrapped and the coaches were making their selections for the Varsity team, I was worried about my lack of a track record but was optimistic that I would be selected for the Varsity team since, as they said, I showed "so much promise."

Sitting across from my coach, I listened as she started to break the news to me:

"Sydney, you have the best attitude of anyone on the team. It has been an absolute pleasure having you around to cheer on the team while you've been injured. If we could keep you on to boost morale for the team, we certainly would."

I felt my eyes glaze over.

"At the end of the day, you're too short to row Varsity."

I looked around. I was surrounded by women who were either teeny tiny and found a spot on the team as a coxswain - the member of the team who sits at the back of the boat, calls commands for the rowers, and steers the boat - or women who were at least 5'9, some towering above me at 6 feet tall. I was too big to be a coxswain because I couldn't fit in that part of the boat. I was too short to match the stroke length and power of my taller teammates.

It crushed me. All of my dreams came crashing down. And for the longest time, I blamed myself for being injured. I was so hard on myself - *"if only you had listened, or asked for help outside of practice, if you lost 20 pounds, maybe you could be a coxswain."* Regardless of the fact that I never wanted to be a coxswain, I just wanted to row.

I stopped hiking and tried to stretch out my hip.

I shouted ahead to Barry to ask how much further we had to go before we go to the campground.

"It's on the other side of this peak!"

I rolled my eyes and sighed to myself, remembering the first hike we did together and mocking him in a sing-song voice, *"it's just around the bend!"*

The last climb before Blackjack campground was aggressive and we kept getting lapped by people who had started behind us, folks I hadn't seen on the trail until they breezed past us on the last climb before the campground.

On that last climb, I repeated a few mantras to myself:

"Right foot, left foot" came in handy when I had to physically grab onto my pants and drag my right leg up the mountain. My hip was in so much pain, I cried through the steps, begging and pleading with my body to continue to carry me up this mountain. Every four steps, I would keel over, as if braced for impact, sobbing and dry heaving. It felt like I was

doing stadiums at KU, running up and down the bleachers for conditioning practice at ungodly hours in the morning. My legs were shaking from working so hard.

"*Right foot,*" I instructed my body, holding on to my pants and pulling my right leg up to meet the left.

"*Left foot,*" I continued, steadying myself before taking a step up with my left leg.

"*Right foot,*" I said, feeling the desire to vomit all the water I'd been chugging.

"*Left foot,*" I pleaded, as I felt tears welling up behind my eyes. Here we go again. Another cycle that feels more like an exorcism than anything I have control over. I had never experienced emotion moving through my body like this. I had never experienced physical pain like this. All the while, we were surrounded by incredible beauty on this island. Between the fields of sage as far as the eye can see, the ocean views, and Barry's random bouts of shouting "PROUD OF YOU" from up ahead of me, I could almost forget about the pain.

We crested the top of the peak and I could see an open field with rolling hills, the antenna on top of Mt. Blackjack, and some small structures.

My heart rate sped up, but I tried not to get my hopes up. I shouted, asking Barry, the island, myself, anyone who has the answer at this point,

"Is that it? Are we almost there?"

As we got closer to the campground, I heard laughter and shouting.

Oh, sweet baby unicorns, we're almost there.

It was literally around the bend. Knowing we were getting close; all of my pain was magnified. I could feel the dirt rubbing between my skin and my socks. There was a teeny tiny pebble in my left shoe that kept kicking around. My back was killing me. I had sweat dripping into my eyes, stinging every time I blink, making my vision blurry. I haven't caught my breath since we left that playground in the middle of the backcountry. All I could think about is how much pain I was in and how hungry I was. I pulled on my bite valve to get a sip of water and it took considerably more effort than before, as these were the last sips of water. I wanted to walk faster, but my hiking boots had transformed into cinder blocks, and it took every last ounce of energy I had to get to our campsite.

We got to the campground and I was relieved to see that our campsite is one of the first ones off the trail. As soon as I sat down, I ripped off my shoes to let my feet air out. My legs were still shaking from the last climb and my pinky toes had turned into blisters. Barry handed me the knife he packed so I can drain them. I squeezed some hand sanitizer into my hand, rubbed it on the tip of the knife, and rubbed some on my toes. I gently poked my heel with my finger, testing the spot I had taped up in the morning. It was a blister now. I pulled off the tape and rubbed some sanitizer on my heel as well. Then, I followed Barry's instructions as he walked me through how to pierce the skin, relieve the pressure, and allow the blisters to drain. I've always had a weird fascination with picking at my feet - whether that's the skin or toenails - and while I was in a tremendous amount of pain, I wasn't squeamish. I was impressed. Captivated. I couldn't look away. This was so gross and so painful and at the same time. The moment the blister started to drain, I felt like a whole new woman.

We put up our tiny tent as I was hobbling around trying to keep my feet clean in the soft dirt. After playing Tetris with our sleeping pads to find a configuration that made sense, we started to make dinner. My first dehydrated meal was absolutely delicious. I selected chicken and dumplings because it was the highest calorie meal I packed. I was exhausted and I couldn't walk another step. I filled up my water and drank it all. I had to pee, but the idea of walking uphill to the bathrooms sounded like my personal hell. I decided I would do it in the morning. By 6:30 p.m. I was lights out, dead to the world, asleep in our tent.

CHAPTER 4

THANKFUL FOR SNAPS

I woke up the next morning, and my legs were stiff beyond belief. The night prior, I wasn't even able to make it uphill to the bathroom once we arrived at Blackjack campground. And now here we were, getting ready for another day on the trail. The only thing that got me out of the tent was the fact that we would be stopping at the Airport in the Sky, and that the trail was mostly downhill into Little Harbor. We had a day off in Little Harbor the next day, so I knew once I got through this section of the trail, I'd be able to rest my weary bones for a full 24 hours before continuing on to Two Harbors.

This was my first breakfast on the trail, and I was really excited about it. I picked the breakfast scramble – a dehydrated mix of eggs, sausage, and hash browns. I really enjoyed the ritual of making breakfast in the backcountry - heating up the water, adding it to the bag, and waiting for it to do what it does. I was famished. We planned to stop at the Airport in the Sky on our way into Little Harbor to get one of the famous buffalo burgers at the DC3 Grill. It was a short two miles from the campground, and I would have already eaten breakfast, but I didn't care. Hiker hunger was real, and after the first day on the trail, my body was begging for calories. Time to eat.

As I opened the bag, I looked inside. It looked like mush but, honestly, it smelled delicious. We had made up a small bag of "camp seasoning" which was everything we usually put on our food at home: salt, black pepper, white pepper, crushed red pepper, granulated garlic, thyme, rosemary, and some cayenne. Without it, it was pretty tasty. With it, oh my goddess. You would think I had never eaten breakfast before. As I had the first bite all mixed up with our added spices, my eyes rolled in the back of my head, as if I had just sunk my teeth into my first double double from In N Out.

"BABE, good choice on the breakfast selections, this is delicious!" I called over to Barry as he prepared his food.

We finished eating, took our time getting dressed, and packed up camp. We set out for Little Harbor.

Climbing out of Blackjack wasn't difficult by any normal standards, but I wasn't operating within a normal standard. My legs were on fire. The blisters appeared to be multiplying. It took everything I had to not whine all the way down into the canyon. I thought downhill was supposed to be easy. I could see the airport building looming. I watched as planes flew into the airport. We made our way past the soapstone, evidence of the Tongva, some of the first people to live on the island. I was unhappy about going downhill. Now my legs were weak and shaking like they did on that last climb before Blackjack the evening prior. I stopped at every switchback to try to catch my breath and chug water. *Will I ever find the balance? Will I ever find flat ground? Will I ever be able to breathe normally? Will I ever be able to hike and NOT be in a tremendous amount of pain?* I paused at some shade before the final path up to the airport and cried. About what, I don't really know, but the frustration and the energy had to go somewhere, and it was coming out of my face.

As I trudged through the final switchbacks, under the sign that welcomes you to the airport, and over to the main building, I was already hungry, even though I had just eaten breakfast. Time to see what this burger was all about.

I saw a bunch of backpacks by the door to the DC3 Grill and followed suit, slinging my pack off my shoulders and once again feeling the sweet release of all the tension, compression, and strain. We swung the doors open like we owned the joint, marched up to the counter, past a stuffed bison head mounted on the wall, and ordered our burgers.

We filled up our water bottles with cold water and found a seat inside near the windows. I wanted to keep an eye on the area where our gear was because I was not about to lose all of that equipment.

Our burgers arrived and I inhaled it like I hadn't had solid food in over a year. I had only eaten two meals out of a bag so far on this trip, but this burger was a gift from heaven. We wandered around the gift store, contemplated getting a cookie for the hike down to Little Harbor, but decided against it and got back on the trail. I slung my pack back over my shoulders, secured my waist belt, secured my chest strap, and found myself checking for my parachute deployment handle, as if my Osprey backpack was my skydiving rig, and I was preparing for a skydive.

Walking back toward the trail, I smiled at the thought of the summer I learned how to skydive.

I'll never forget the night I met Barry - June 11, 2010. I had opted to do a Friday night first jump course – the ground training required before you make your first jump in the Accelerated Freefall (AFF) program. I read that this would take 6-8 hours for a typical student. The day before my course, I got a Facebook message from this guy named Barry, who said he was the school manager for Freefall University, the student program at Chicagoland Skydiving Center. He asked what time I planned to arrive, indicating that if I could get there early, we could get done early.

The Blackhawks had just won the Stanley Cup and the parade was scheduled for Friday afternoon. I was working at one of the largest global PR firms in their Chicago office, so most of the folks on my teams were planning to attend, thus, making it possible for me to leave early. I had driven to the office and parked in a garage so I could drive straight out to the drop zone, my anticipation building all day long. When it was quitting time, I got in my car, plugged the address for the DZ in my GPS, and made my way west out of the city to a little town off Highway 30 called Hinckley. I got out of town just in time, before traffic got wild and all the streets shut down for the parade. As I pulled off the main highway to get on Highway 30, I started seeing familiar sights from the weekend before when I made a tandem skydive. First, passing through Aurora. Then Big Rock. Then Hinckley. As I pulled into the gravel lot, my heart started racing.

For the first time in a long time, I was choosing something for me. Not because my parents suggested I try it, not because my friends were doing it, because I really, truly wanted to, and I didn't care if I didn't know anyone there. I felt empowered as I got out of the car, walking toward what I hoped would be a very exciting chapter of my life.

If I only knew what I was getting myself into.

Once I parked, I took a deep breath. I had been blasting Kelly Clarkson on the drive out to the country to get pumped up, and I let the song finish playing before I got out of the car, not wanting to interrupt the empowerment session. I'm superstitious like that. I took off my seatbelt, grabbed the skydiver's logbook they had given me the weekend prior, and walked to the small aircraft hangar where I was told to meet Barry. As I stepped over the short fence between the parking lot and the courtyard, I stumbled, feet-knees-face, into the grass near the volleyball court.

Shit. This is a sport that requires at least some level of body awareness, and I just crashed and burned, not even five steps into this experience. *Shit shit shit shit shit.*

I dusted myself off and looked around. *Did anyone see that?* The place was mostly empty. Only a red Jeep Wrangler in the lot and a black Range Rover. I saw a guy sitting on the picnic tables – tall and lanky, sun-weathered skin, smoking a cigarette.

"Excuse me, do you know where I can find Barry?" I asked.

He motioned to the hangar behind him.

I stepped inside and saw Barry.

He was about my height, and I'm 5'4 on a good day. I saw a tattoo on his calf, and one that wrapped around his ankle. He walked over and introduced himself.

"Hi, I'm Barry" he said, extending his hand for a handshake. His eyes were kind, his smile friendly, his demeanor confident.

I reached out and shook his hand, "Sydney, nice to meet you."

The rest of the evening was a blur. He showed me the equipment I would be using, pointing out all of the components that would save my life. We talked about what we would do on this skydive. He took me over to the parked airplane and we talked about safety around an aircraft. He explained the structure built to represent an airplane door and showed me how to position myself to exit the aircraft safely. We talked about emergency procedures - what happens when your parachute malfunctions, and how to handle it. It was a lot of information.

I'm an active listener and I like to confirm my understanding by nodding and saying "uh-huh" or something affirmative to show I am comprehending the information. At one point in time, Barry looked at me and asked,

"Are you actually listening or just nodding and saying 'uh-huh'?"

"Oh, I'm listening," I retorted.

The final portion of this ground training was a written exam. Being the gold-star-earning, good-grade-getting student I was, I got all of them right except for one. He told me that he had been teaching skydiving for more than a decade and that I was the shortest ground school he had ever taught – we were done in less than four hours. And he said he hadn't ever had a student do so well on the test. He was impressed, I could tell.

That night, I drove back home to my apartment in the city, and something felt different. I figured it was excitement and nerves around doing my first jump with my own parachute on my back. Little did I know; I just met the man I would choose to spend the rest of my life with.

Back in the present moment on the trail, I smiled to myself and felt my eyes well up at the memory of that fateful day. Here we were, six years later, married for four years, and we were a few miles into our second day of this grand adventure together. We passed the sign that pointed us back onto the Trans-Catalina Trail. We had been hiking for about five, maybe 10 minutes before I felt a rumble in my guts. It was too far to run back to the airport. This was an emergency.

I was going to shit my pants.

I called ahead to Barry, alerting him. We had a bit of a situation. This trail is open, exposed, and there's very little coverage or bushes to squat behind. I looked around and found a place that was out of view from any of the fire access roads where they host the eco-tours of the island. I was squeezing my butt cheeks together and squirming as I took off my backpack, found a place to squat, fumbled with my pants, thankful for snaps instead of buttons, and got my pants down just in time to not soil myself.

No no no no no, this can't be happening! I thought. *What is happening here? Why am I peeing out of my butt? Why does this have to happen right now? Is this the end of it?* I did not anticipate this variable.

I didn't have time to dig a hole. Thankfully Barry had picked up some napkins when we were at the airport so he could blow his nose. When I was done, I stood up, waddled away from the poop on this sloping hill, and pulled my pants up.

I did my best to cover the poop by kicking some of the dirt around it on top of it and covering it with some rocks. I had a big bag of jerky in my pack and a small bag of it that I was keeping in my hip pocket for easy access, so I emptied the small bag into the big one and tucked my poop napkin into the small bag. I had basically failed at leaving no trace, but I did my best in an emergency situation.

We kept hiking, and another 15 minutes later, same thing. Another emergency situation. Exact same routine. Scramble to find a place out of view from the fire roads above and below us, scramble to get my pack off, rush to pull my pants down before I shit myself.

"WHAT THE FUUUUUUUUCK?" I screamed silently in my head as I was squatting.

Barry and I both had the burger, why was my body doing this? Why was he not also shitting his brains out all over this trail?

I cleaned myself up and made my way back to the trail where Barry was keeping watch. We continued our descent into Little Harbor, our first of three beach campsites on this trip.

On the way down, we turned onto a "trail" called Sheep Chute Road. It was deeply eroded, and it was steep. At one point, Barry started hiking backward downhill to protect his knees. I had to pull over to address one of my pinky toe blisters, and in the process of removing my sock, I ripped off the tape from the blister on my heel, taking the skin with it. Now I had several miles on this steep road, sock rubbing on raw skin, feeling like I wrapped my ankle with sandpaper. Turns out downhill all day isn't my jam. My knees were killing me, and I found myself wishing I was a sheep. I figured if I had four legs, maybe this wouldn't hurt so bad. That visual made me laugh and gave me a second wind.

We finally made it into Little Harbor, and it was everything the videos and pictures showed and then some. Crystal clear blue water, a sailboat bobbing in the waves in the harbor, a rock formation that looked like a whale's tail, another harbor off to the left, and campsites right on the beach. We found our campsite, complete with a box for our food and gear, a picnic table, and a shade structure. We took care of our gear, and I made my way down to the water, limping as I went. I was worried about what my heel blister would look like.

Barry grabbed the GoPro as we went down to the water, and before I walked into the ocean, I took off my sock for the camera, revealing my blister. I walked over to the beach to rinse and soak my feet in the cold ocean water. I walked in slowly and stood to where the water would wash over my feet, not submerging them. This water was freezing, and I was not ready for it.

I had to coax myself to walk out further into the surf, but eventually I made my way to calf-deep, then up to my knees. That was as far as I was willing to go, you couldn't pay me to go any deeper. I walked back over toward Barry, grabbed my towel, and waddled back to our campsite, excited about having a whole day in this island paradise to do whatever I wanted. In this case, what I wanted was to do absolutely nothing.

Mission: Accomplished.

Our day off was the ultimate lazy day - most of which I spent watching life go by. After we made breakfast, I hobbled down to the ocean to soak my feet. When I returned to camp, I set up shop on the picnic table.

Before we left for this trip, Barry thought it was ridiculous to pack my tarot cards. He joked about them every time I said my feet hurt, insinuating that if I hadn't brought them along, I wouldn't have blisters. That the difference between total blister town and healthy, happy feet was completely dependent on whether or not one had a tarot deck on their person.

I sat on that picnic table for hours, asking different questions of the Universe and myself, pulling tarot cards, journaling about what the cards meant. All the while, we were watching a bison make its way through the campsites and canyon behind us. Bison? On an island? Yes. Back in the 1920's, a Western movie was filmed on the island. The bison that they brought over from the mainland were never returned to their homes after they finished filming, the production crew just left them on the island. So now there are more than 100 bison freely roaming the island. I had never seen one up close before, and I certainly didn't want them to come any closer, but the bison we saw around the island were truly majestic to watch in their natural habitat.

As night fell, we talked about the plan for the next day. We heard the forecasts of rain but having lived in Southern California for more than five years at that point and being able to count any significant rainstorms in the region on one hand, we weren't holding our breath.

We only brought Barry's ultralight tent. The product description said it's big enough for two people, but as my legs started cramping in the middle of our first night on the trail, I wondered how they're measuring humans for this tent. One adult and a newborn? Sure. Two six-year-olds? Maybe. Two adults? Seems like a stretch. Barry and I are both 5'4" on a good day. Height-wise, we should not feel so cramped in here, but this tent tapers to a point by our feet. Lying in that tent, I was 70 pounds heavier than I am present day, and as I wiggled around trying to find a comfortable position, I got a bit breathless. I finally found a position that didn't cause me pain or induce cramping and I drifted back to sleep, the waves from the ocean providing the ultimate white noise machine. This was the life.

CHAPTER 5

I CAN DO HARD THINGS

Around midnight I heard a loud crash. I woke from a deep sleep, sitting straight up in the tent.

"*WHAT WAS THAT?*" I shouted.

Barry sat up in a daze. I panicked, and my first assumption was that we were being attacked by bison.

I wiped my eyes and rubbed my face, trying to catch my breath. Once I figured out where I was and what was happening, I realized it was raining. The loud crash was thunder, not a bison coming to wake us up for a midnight cuddle puddle.

I hadn't been in a thunderstorm like this since we lived in Illinois, and I certainly had never experienced rain like this in a tent. This wasn't really part of the plan, and my groggy brain was having a hard time.

"What do we do? Where do we go? Are we safe?" I asked.

"It's just a little rain, everything is going to be okay," Barry replied.

I had to pee. Great. The last thing I wanted to do was wear my too-tight shoes and slosh through puddles to get to the porta potty across the campground.

I grabbed Barry's shoes, put them on my feet, and unzipped the tent.

"Just a little rain?" I asked nobody in particular.

As I looked outside, I saw water rushing down to our campsite. We had opted to sleep underneath a tree, and I was regretting that decision. A moat was forming around our tent, there were bison prints right outside of the tent that were full of water. It reminded me of that scene in Jurassic Park where they're in the Jeep and Jeff Goldblum has a cup of water, and you can see the water ripple and vibrate as the T-Rex is approaching from the forest.

I looked out toward where the porta potty was. Hopefully nobody else had to go right now. If I made my way out of this tent without soaking these shoes to the sole, that would be a miracle. If I had to stand and wait for someone to finish up, I'd be done for.

I couldn't run, because there were too many puddles to navigate. The gravel road that separated us from the toilets was turning into a mud pit. But I didn't have a choice, I had to go. And after the shitstorm on the way down to Little Harbor, I didn't trust a fart.

I unzipped the tent the rest of the way, wished Barry a nice rest of his life in case I got gored by a bison on the way to the porta potty, and clumsily crawled over him to get outside.

I half tip-toed, half hopped around the puddles, navigating the distance between tent and toilet like a battlefield. Every military battle scene in every movie I've ever watched was now coming to life. I had visions of tucking and rolling to avoid a rogue eagle, as if the eagles would be swooping humans in a thunderstorm. I imagined a bison waiting for me outside of the porta potty when I was ready to return to the tent, unsure if he was offering a ride or if he was challenging me to a duel. When I finally made it to the bathroom, I clumsily fumbled for a toilet seat cover and held my breath, assuming this would be the most disgusting porta potty of all time.

Once I sat down and got my wits about me, I realized I was wrong. It was dry inside. Clean. The sound of the rain on the plastic roof was oddly soothing. I wondered if I could just wait out the storm. Mother Nature had other plans for me, and waiting it out wouldn't be one of them, because as soon as I thought about that, I heard more rain. Louder. Another crash of thunder.

It was getting worse. I had to get back to the tent.

Making my way back to my cozy sleeping bag was less treacherous, but still scary. I slipped and slid all around the muddy bits. I felt these shoes becoming heavier with accumulated mud, causing my calves and shins to cramp up. I danced and hopped and tip-toed back to the tent, and when I arrived, I was exhausted. I unzipped the tent, turned around, and sat down in it backward, with my feet hanging out of the tent. I didn't want to bring these muddy shoes into the tent, so I took them off and tucked them under the rainfly, hoping they wouldn't get any worse between now and the morning.

I wiggled my way over Barry and back into my sleeping bag, checking the tent for any leaks. We were fine, for now. As long as I wasn't getting wet, I could handle this. I started to tell Barry about the battlefield between tent and toilet and drifted back to sleep to the sound of rain on the tent.

I slept for another few hours. By the time we woke up, the rain had stopped, and we emerged from the tent to assess the situation. As we moved around the campground, we sloshed around in the mud. I tried to keep my pack on the bench of the picnic table so it wouldn't get soaked in a puddle. As we were gearing up to leave, it started raining again. I started whining and stomping around like a toddler (one of my better qualities) and Barry offered me his rain gear. My biggest fear was getting wet and then getting cold, so I accepted.

After I put on the rain gear, the ranger pulled up to us in his truck. We asked him about the trail conditions, and I was half inclined to ask him for a ride to Two Harbors. He told us that the conditions were similar to what we were experiencing here at camp, but that it was still safe to hike. The access roads, however, weren't in great shape. He warned us that if we decided to proceed and something happened that required a rescue, it would take some extra time to get someone out to us. Our choice.

We could wait it out, or we could keep going. We could keep going, or we could get a ride.

We decided to keep going and passed on the ride.

As we made our way out of the campground, the rain had stopped, and the clouds broke. I was wearing the rain gear for approximately 20 minutes before I took it off again. Between the midnight wake up bathroom run and this morning's costume change, I was frustrated and cranky.

I lifted my head to check out the views. There was a path that looked like it was going straight up. No switchbacks to make the climb easier, just straight elevation gain. The grade of the trail plus the soft, rocky terrain felt unstable at best. I struggled to keep my feet underneath me, each step squishing and twisting at the end of the stride. Every step felt like more effort than the last.

"Shifting down a gear!" Barry shouted back to me.

I giggled and sighed. *Would this ever get easier?*

I keeled over with my hands on my knees, trying to catch my breath and give my legs a rest.

"PROUD OF YOU!" Barry called out.

"PROUD OF ME, TOO!" I shouted back.

I continued climbing up the ridgeline of this peak, up and over pieces of white quartz peppered with pinky orange streaks. This entire peak consisted of this stone; it was breathtaking. I kept huffing, kept puffing, cresting over false peak after false peak. As my socks grated on open blisters like sandpaper, I started to cry.

I paused to collect my thoughts. We had hiked almost 22 miles across the island at this point. We made it through the longest day, made it through a rainstorm, and we were still here. I was still here. I wasn't sure I'd be able to do this, but I was doing it.

"I can do hard things," I whimpered.

It felt like an admission. A confession, even. For so long, I had been dumbing myself down, trying to find a box to fit into. More specifically, a smaller body to fit into. For as long as I could remember, I had been nitpicky about my body, uncomfortable in my own skin. In the months leading up to this trip, I had turned a corner. Instead of mindlessly scrolling and having a passive experience, I started to use social media intentionally. I stopped following things that made me feel bad about myself. I followed accounts that featured beautiful outdoor photography. I unfollowed brands that only showed me a thin, white standard of beauty and started seeking out body positive accounts, activists who celebrated women of all shapes, all races, all abilities. As my feed diversified, so did my opinions of myself. When I was in the dressing room in Encinitas picking up gear for this trip, I had asked myself how we got here. What happened that led to me standing in front of a mirror in a body I didn't recognize?

I didn't have the answers yet, but before I got on this trail, I had moved away from *hating* my body. Now I was simply indifferent, and after a lifetime of negative self-talk, indifferent was better than hate.

I kept hiking through the pain.

I can do hard things. I chanted this to myself with every step. It felt like a second wind. *I can do hard things* became my mantra up one of the toughest climbs of this trail so far.

The rest of the hike from Little Harbors to Two Harbors was a mix of steep climbs followed by super narrow stretches, slip-sliding through muddy patches, and some of the most intense pain I had experienced yet on the trail. The combination of soggy socks and the mud that had accumulated on the bottom of my hiking shoes was oppressive. As we made our way on the final descent into Two Harbors, my muddy boots started to pick up loose gravel. It felt like my feet turned into cinder blocks once again, and my legs were spaghetti.

By the time we arrived in town, we weren't sure where to go. We took a left toward Catalina Harbor and thankfully, a kind couple out for a walk noticed our backpacks and asked us if we needed help. They pointed us in the right direction and told us that camper check-in was on the dock.

We limped our way through town, arriving at the Two Harbors dock to check in. I couldn't see a campground. Were we in the right place? I made my way to the little office and asked about where the campground was. I pulled out my reservation paperwork and looked around again. The young man on duty showed me a map. The campground was another mile or so uphill.

Nope. Not interested. I thought. After the day we had, the idea of walking further uphill to sleep in a soggy tent was not doing it for me. The next day, we planned to hike out to Starlight Beach, out near the very edge of the island, then into Parsons Landing, our last campground on this journey. The last night was another remote beach campground. It faces the mainland and we were looking forward to watching fireworks up and down the coast from the comfort of our campsite on the beach.

I asked about the trail conditions for the last leg of the trail.

"We'll make the call in the morning," he said.

This was my first backpacking trip. I didn't know what that meant, and he could tell.

"The trail is in a questionable condition," he continued. "Depending on how much rain we get tonight, it's possible that the trail won't be passable tomorrow. We'll make the call in the morning."

Well, my body is in a questionable condition, I thought to myself. I thanked him for the information, and I went back out to talk to Barry.

We had a couple of options here. We could make our way up to the campsite and hope it didn't rain. Our gear was already soggy from the night before and my legs were completely exhausted, so I wasn't jazzed about that option. They also had these little camping cabins and a community kitchen back behind the restaurant. Nothing fancy, just two beds with plastic-coated mattresses, a door that locks, and a fridge. With your cabin reservation, you also had access to the showers.

I was really honest about how I was feeling and how much pain I was in. I didn't try to sugarcoat it, and I didn't "suck it up" and ignore what my body was telling me. I was in excruciating pain between my blisters and sore legs, and Barry's knee was still bothering him from the descent into Little Harbor. Even if the trail was magically in pristine condition, I wasn't confident that my body would be able to get me to the next campground. After a quick deliberation, Barry and I called it. We traded in our Parsons Landing reservations for a camping cabin in Two Harbors for two nights. We would celebrate New Year's with the locals and the other hikers attempting to complete this trail.

We tossed our stuff in the room and on our way to the showers, we ran into the couple that pointed us in the right direction. They were our neighbors! After a little small talk, I expressed my dire need for a shower, and we made a beeline for the bathhouse.

After four days on the trail and in the worst pain of my life, the shower was absolute heaven. This was the longest I had gone without a shower since Adam died, and by the time the water warmed up and I stepped in,

I felt like I was in an Herbal Essences commercial. I took tender care of my feet, making sure they were clean. As I stood under the hot water, I reflected on how far we had come. Just a few short days ago, I didn't know if I could do this. Standing here in this shower, I congratulated myself for hiking more than 26 miles of this trail. While I didn't finish it, I did know one thing: I love my body.

I took this time in the shower to thank each part of my body that made this trek possible. I started with my feet - my poor, blister-covered feet. I thanked them for their service and apologized for thinking that standing at my standing desk was the same as breaking in hiking boots. I thanked my calves, my massive, swollen, tender-to-the-touch calves for driving me up ridgelines and keeping me steady. I've always loved my legs, and I thanked them profusely. My legs haven't worked this hard since I was on the rowing team at KU, and I was extra grateful for their ability to hang in there and keep me going. I thanked my shoulders and my arms for their strength in carrying a very heavy backpack across an island. Finally, I touched my stomach.

My stomach has been the source of so much anxiety and shame. I noticed toward the end of the trip that my pants were a bit looser. I had to sausage squeeze into the biggest pants that store sold for this trip, and by the end of it, they fit relatively comfortably. Instead of viewing my stomach as a mess that needs to be fixed, a part of my body that is unworthy of love and touch unless it's flat and muscular like all of the athletes, models, and celebrities I admired growing up, I made a shift. I have long referred to my mid-section as my gut in a negative way. Like a beer belly, versus intuition. In the shower, after this journey, after admitting to myself that I can do hard things, I apologized to my stomach. I apologized for demonizing this part of my body. I apologized to myself for how poorly I've spoken about myself, about my appearance, for placing so much worth on the appearance of one particular part of my body. I put one hand on my belly, one hand on my heart, and cried hot tears in that hot shower.

"I knew I could trust you," I said, looking down at my stomach.

This thick, powerful, beautiful part of my body - my gut, my intuition, my inner knowing, my center - has kept me safe and alive for my life thus far. It was worth celebrating, not criticizing. After I finished my shower, I took another good long look at myself in the mirror.

"I love my body, and I can do hard things."

I returned back to our camping cabin where Barry was waiting for me. I felt refreshed, renewed, empowered, and proud. I was also a bit disappointed that we wouldn't finish the trail on this trip.

"TO THE BAR!!" he shouted.

We made our way down to the Harbor Reef Saloon, the bar attached to the Harbor Reef Restaurant. As we scanned the menu, I saw a drink called Buffalo Milk. I remembered one of our skydiving buddies saying that Buffalo Milk was the signature drink of the island and that we had to get one when we got to Two Harbors, so we ordered two of them straight away.

After four days on the trail, this drink was everything I didn't know I needed. It's frozen, and it tastes like a mudslide with some banana liqueur added in. Topped with whipped cream and freshly grated nutmeg, it's a dream. As we sucked down these delicious cocktails, trying our best to avoid a brain freeze, we scanned the rest of the menu.

This place had a buffalo burger, a regular burger, and the Harbor Reef Burger - a blend of buffalo and Kobe beef. Considering I turned this island into my litter box after the buffalo burger I had at the airport, I was hesitant. As if on cue, a server walked by with a burger and my eyes followed that server across the bar to the other side where happy hikers were patiently waiting. I might have actually drooled, because the bartender caught me staring down the server and told me that was the Harbor Reef Burger.

I decided it was worth the risk, and we both ordered a Harbor Reef Burger. My first Buffalo Milk was already down the hatch, so we ordered another round. When the burgers arrived, it was game time. I had been eating food out of a bag for the last four days, and I was ready for something fresh that didn't need to be rehydrated.

That first bite of the burger was like the first moments of that shower - absolute bliss. I was overcome with endorphins and my eyes rolled all the way back in my head. Was this the best burger I've ever had or is this how food tastes after days on end of dehydrated meals? Probably a little bit of both.

I looked at Barry, he was having the same experience. I paused and took it all in.

We did it.

"We're going to have to come back here and do the whole trail, you know that, right?" I said.

"Oh, for sure. As long as we can get these burgers again."

CHAPTER 6

OAR LOCKS

few months after we got home from the first hike on the Trans-Catalina Trail, I went to Paris with my best friend, Kat. She attended culinary school at Le Cordon Bleu and hadn't been back since graduation, so she was doing a little Paris reunion trip, and I decided to crash it.

I had only travelled internationally with my family, and with Barry for our honeymoon, so this was going to be a new experience to travel solo to meet my friend. We explored a bunch of options for what we wanted to do and where we wanted to go when I got there, but we were keeping things loose. The No-Plan Plan is one of our favorite ways to explore, whether that's at home or abroad. This trip was going to be epic.

When I landed in Paris, I had arranged for a ride to the apartment where we were staying for the next 10 days. I found my driver, got in the car, and took in the sights. The streets were as charming as I thought they would be. As we weaved in and out of traffic on our way to the apartment, I looked out the window wistfully. I missed Barry and wished I could be sharing this with him, too.

When I arrived at the address, Kat met me downstairs. We got in the old-school elevator and made our way up to the apartment. One of our skydiving friends owned this flat, and it was spectacular. I walked in and fell in love with the natural light. I had heard a lot of complaints from international travelers, saying that the accommodations in Europe were teeny tiny compared to those in the US – but this flat didn't fit that bill. The kitchen was gorgeous, well-appointed, and opened up to the living room. Kat showed me where she was staying, then showed me back to my room. She pulled open the curtains and there it was – the Eiffel Tower. For the next 10 days, every time I wake up, before I go to bed, at ANY time, I had a view of this iconic tower. The whole thing felt like a dream.

I had taken a red eye to get there and was starving, it was time to explore. On our way to breakfast, we passed a storefront called San Diego Boot Company. What are the chances? We traveled all the way from San Diego here to Paris, and here was a boot store of all things. We laughed, trying to recall anyone we know who would wear boots in San Diego. When we arrived at breakfast, I was so ready.

I ordered a latte, scrambled eggs, and a croissant. These croissants were the real deal. Crisp and flaky on the outside, soft and chewy on the inside. I was in heaven. This breakfast alone was worth the trip. What else was possible while we were here?

We walked eleven miles around the city that first day, and when we got back, jet lag took me down. We planned to go to the Bastille Market in the morning, and we'd take the Metro to get there. All of my international travel prior to this trip was via cruise ship. So even if we were in a country where I didn't speak the language, the crew did, and if we were onshore, chances are we were on a tour with an English-speaking guide. In Paris, on the Metro, we were the only folks speaking English.

As I looked around, I saw a sea of diversity. People of all shapes, sizes, races, and abilities. I had a very narrow expectation of Paris: runway models smoking cigarettes while drinking espresso or fine wine. High fashion. Fancy perfume. And don't get me wrong, I found all of those things while in Paris too, but that first day on the Metro was inspiring.

When I wasn't surrounded with English speakers, I found myself alone with my thoughts. I couldn't understand what they were saying. They could have been calling me an ugly American cow and I wouldn't have known. This felt a lot like when I was on the Trans-Catalina Trail for the first time. Without an international data plan, I wasn't scrolling through the news or social media, so I didn't have this perpetual reminder of how the world is melting down. I looked around at the media these Parisians were consuming. Some were reading books, most had headphones in, but there wasn't a single trashy magazine on the train. No judgments being made about the female form, zooming in on a celebrity's body at the beach, nit-picking cellulite and baby bumps. As Kat and I counted down the stops until it was time to disembark, I found peace.

We made our way to Bastille Market and the sights and smells were incredible. We stopped at an oyster counter and I ate oysters that were harvested earlier that morning, washing it down with a crisp white wine. At an olive stand, we tried every variety while the purveyor of the olives hit on Kat and told us how beautiful we were. When he asked where we were from, we told him California, and he started singing "California Girls." We picked up cheeses and meats and fruits and planned to have the most epic feast when we got home.

We returned to the apartment, got in the elevator, and when we got out, I noticed a full-length mirror in the entryway. I grabbed Kat and we posed for a mirror selfie. This became our tradition for the rest of the trip. Every time we walked past the mirror; we'd snap a selfie. Prior to the first TCT trip, I had been hiding in photos. If Barry and I were out and wanted to take a photo, I'd sneak behind him, wrap my arms around his shoulders, and nuzzle my head onto his shoulder. I never let my full body be seen. I don't have many pictures in general from these years of my life, but when we were in Paris, it was a whole different ball game.

I felt confident, like I did on the trail. For the next 10 days, this cycle would repeat. Get on the Metro, observe the beauty of humanity in all of its forms, feel beautiful myself in the absence of societal messaging telling me I'm not, take a full-body selfie, celebrate life with my best friend. I walked around that city like I owned the joint. I did not expect to feel like a goddess in Paris - this city where I assumed everyone would be thin, white, and chic - but I did.

When I returned from Paris, I felt refreshed, energized, renewed. That much time alone with my positive thoughts was heaven sent. When I got home, I rushed into Barry's arms and told him everything about the trip. He could tell something had shifted, and he was happy to see me happy.

Once the jetlag wore off, Barry suggested we go paddleboarding.

We had never been paddleboarding before but had been discussing it for a while before I left for Paris. I thought we'd rent boards and check it out. Nope, a local paddleboard company was having a warehouse sale and we were going all in.

I was excited about the prospect of getting out on the water – this made me feel like an official Southern California gal. It's practically required of San Diego residents to own paddleboards; we were finally becoming real locals!

After we picked up the boards, we made our way to the store to get the necessary accessories and safety equipment. We found stuff sacks to keep our personal belongings dry, tried on lifejackets, and as we were getting ready to leave, I realized I didn't have a swimsuit that fit. I hadn't been swimsuit shopping in over a decade.

I walked back to the swimsuit section and picked up a one piece. White with horizontal navy stripes. I grabbed an XL and a large, the last sizes on the rack, and mentally crossed my fingers. I closed the door behind me, locked it, and paused. I looked at myself in the mirror. I hadn't lost any weight since we hiked the Trans-Catalina Trail the year prior. I remembered my pledge to honor my inner athlete and was satisfied that we were taking this step. It was summer now and hiking in Southern California is miserable in the heat. I leaned into the inner athlete thing and determined that my life now consisted of paddleboarding season and hiking season. When it's too hot to hike, I'd be on the water. When the water is too cold, I'd be on the trail.

I took off my clothes and tried on the large suit first. Camel toe. No go. Abort mission.

I wiggled out of the large and into the XL. It fit perfectly.

For the first time in my life, swimsuit shopping wasn't traumatic. In fact, it was empowering. As I stood there in this suit with horizontal stripes - breaking all the fashion rules - I smiled. Continuing the self-love fest from that first shower after hiking 26 miles, every part of my body that I had previously criticized was now getting love, affection, and appreciation.

GIRRRRRRRRRL, I said to myself. *Your butt looks delicious in this suit. Your tattoos are gorgeous – you should show those off more. I know you're not planning on having kids, but you are capable of creating life, you're a powerhouse for humanity.*

I waved my hands around my stomach region and snapped my fingers at myself – my gut was right, I could trust it, and it looked INCREDIBLE in this suit.

I stood up on my tippy toes. This time, not to suck in and see what my smaller body could look like, but to check out my calves. They still had quite a bit of definition from the hike and from all the walking I did in Paris. *Yep, best legs in this town, that's for sure!*

I emerged from the dressing room proudly clutching this one piece. This shopping trip was a game changer in its own right, and I started to wonder if the dressing room was actually a magical portal for self-love and acceptance.

Not missing a beat, we made a beeline for the San Diego Bay. We unpacked our boards and started inflating them. Doing this by hand was a workout in itself, and I was exhausted before we got on the boards. Once they were fully inflated, we headed down to the water.

They call it standup paddleboarding but let's be honest, I was on my knees at first. There was no way I'd be able to stand up on this thing, not yet. We paddled out toward a little island in a cove, and when we got there, we took a break. Looking around, I felt the calmest I had felt in a very long time. What was this? I like it.

I heard the sound of oars locking in place before I saw them. I instantly connected the dots between my calm and the "why" as a rowing team from one of the local universities passed us.

Oh riiiiight, I was on the women's rowing team at the University of Kansas.

I smiled and cheered and reflected on some of my favorite times on the water with the team. My affinity for water was part of the calm, yes, but that didn't feel like the whole answer. We kept paddling and when we slowed down to a stop at the next resting place, it hit me.

As true as it is that my skin is white and my thumbs look like toes, I maintained a deeply held belief that was challenged in this moment: I believed that if I had the *audacity* to go out in public in a swimsuit and didn't cover up my body, people would be so offended by my appearance that they would drop dead. So, considering the absence of floating bodies in the San Diego Bay, and having witnessed the rowing team doing sprints as they passed us, it all made sense.

The water is my happy place, and I've been robbing myself of this experience for more than a decade. If it was possible that folks didn't die at the sight of my body in a swimsuit, what other lies have I been feeding myself?

For the rest of the summer, we paddled as often as we could. Early mornings were our favorite, it was a great way to start the day and the water was like glass before the afternoon winds kicked up. We did sunset paddle sessions, hauling firewood on our boards from the dock, across the bay to Fiesta Island. After sunset, we would light a fire and just relax until the fire burned out. We did several full moon sessions, too. By the light of our headlamps, the stars, and the moon, we navigated around the glassy bay in the dark, the only folks out there enjoying that experience. It was one of the most magical summers of my life.

In early September, we launched from Spanish Landing, a park near the airport in San Diego, and paddled around the downtown side of the bay to observe the Tall Ships. It was a long session, and the weather was not the San Diego standard – 72 and sunny. Nope, this day it was Florida hot – temperatures exceeding 90 degrees and the air was so thick it was hard to breathe. I didn't bring enough water and we were out there for one of the longer sessions we had done since we got the boards. When we got back, I was dehydrated and exhausted. For the next two weeks, I didn't feel right. I thought maybe I had heat exhaustion, perhaps even mild heatstroke. I had some serious stomach issues and chalked it up to the water fountain at the park – maybe I caught some kind of virus or something.

I woke up on September 18, 2017 in excruciating pain. It felt like someone had taken a corset, shoved it into my mid-section through my belly button, wrapped it around my intestines, cinching it down, tightening around all my internal organs. It was awful. My first thought was appendicitis and I got scared. I told Barry what was happening, and we rushed over to urgent care.

Once I checked in and was called back to the exam room, everything was a blur. The folks at the hospital didn't seem to be interested in the story as to what led to these symptoms, they were just interested in the symptoms themselves. The first nurse I spoke to said I probably had Crohn's disease.

What the hell? Adam, my friend who died on the BASE jump, was living with Crohn's disease, and I knew from his lived experience, his descriptions of what his life was like while managing that disease, that what I was experiencing was NOT what he had. I was flabbergasted that a nurse would jump to a chronic diagnosis. After they did a full blood draw, they sent me home with supplies to collect stool samples to rule out any viruses or parasites. For three days, I pooped into a plastic container I put over the toilet, scooped out a little bit, and put it in a vial with some kind of solution. I returned the samples to the lab after my third poop and scoop. Later that day, as I was pulling into the arrivals section at San Diego International Airport to pick up a friend I haven't seen in a while, I received a call from the hospital.

This is not the best place to receive test results, I thought. I answered the phone reluctantly.

"Hi, Mrs. Williams?"

"Speaking."

The person on the other end introduced themselves as a nurse from my doctor's office. My test results were in.

"You have Type 2 Diabetes," she said.

CHAPTER 7

BIG LEATHER CHAIR

I felt tears sting my eyes. My heart rate quickened. I thanked them for the information and hung up.

My mind was racing.

"Don't wreck the car," was my first thought.

I didn't know what this disease was. I didn't know what was happening inside of my body. All I knew about diabetes was the stigma – I had heard "diabeetus" jokes over the course of my life. The stigma around diabetes told me that fat, lazy, morbidly obese people get it. Old people get it. Your feet can fall off. But I didn't know why this was happening to me. Was this hereditary? Could I cure it? Would I be living with this for the rest of my life? How did we get here?

"Well, I guess I can't eat bread anymore?" I thought to myself.

I was crying at this point, trying to hold it together, not wreck the car, and safely pick up our friend. Barry looked at me and told me we'd figure it out. That everything would be okay. I wanted to believe him. I wiped my face as we pulled up to the curb to pick up our friend. Pleasantries were exchanged, and not surprisingly, he was starving after the flight from Chicago.

We made our way toward the beach to our favorite sandwich shop. As I read the menu options, I was overwhelmed. What did this food do to my body? Did this make my blood sugar better or worse? What can I eat? I figured I was already diabetic, and one more sandwich wasn't going to make or break it, so I got my usual; a turkey club, bacon extra crispy, with avocado. We grabbed the sandwiches to go and walked across the street to enjoy them on the beach. We found a bench on the cliffs near the Pacific Beach pier and I held up my sandwich to the sky, toasting to what I imagined would be my last meal that included bread.

In my mind, I had a little dialogue with my last sandwich, shedding a single tear as I held it up to the sky:

Hey bread. It's Sydney. I think we need to break up. It's not you, it's me. Thank you for all of the energy, nourishment, and comfort you've provided over the years. I just got diagnosed with Type 2 Diabetes, so I'm pretty sure we can't hang out anymore. Thank you for being such a pleasurable part of my life, but I'm afraid we have to part ways now. See ya later, carbs!

The adjustment into managing diabetes was excruciating. On our anniversary, Barry and I went to Juniper and Ivy, one of our favorite restaurants in San Diego. Richard Blais from "Top Chef" opened this restaurant as one of his experimental kitchens, and it is one of our go-to places to take out of town guests or celebrate special occasions.

Sitting at the table, looking at the menu, I started to cry. I was in the process of figuring out which foods were contributing to my elevated blood sugar and which ones were helping keep it stable, and sitting at a corner table, I was overcome with deep sadness.

Throughout my entire life, food has been an expression of love. My father grew up around the restaurant industry and worked in hospitality through his twenties and into his thirties. He taught me how to cook and some of my favorite childhood memories were made in the kitchen. I took to cooking quickly, and when I worked in restaurants to put myself through college, I developed a palate for fine dining and great wine.

Barry also loves cooking, and spending time in the kitchen together was how we celebrated and shared our love for each other. Barry loves any reason to get creative with food and beverages and loves to create a whole menu around a specific theme. As I got older and life started getting harder, cooking was my escape. When the world was just too much, I'd find myself picking an elaborate recipe that I could get lost in.

In my most important relationships, food is a centerpiece. A safe space. A creative outlet. What was diabetes going to do to that part of my life?

I looked up from my menu at Barry, who had reached out for my hand. I was afraid to take his hand because if I had the slightest bit of human touch, I'd turn into a puddle. My defenses would be completely down, and I would have no energy left to retain the tears welling up behind my eyes.

I grabbed his hand and let the tears fall.

"Is this what the rest of my life is going to be like? Crying over menus? Unable to celebrate with food anymore?" I asked.

He squeezed my hand and assured me everything was going to be okay.

As time went on, it got easier. Thankfully the hospital had a great diabetes education program - and honestly, I hope every hospital does, because this is an epidemic. In my classes at the hospital, I learned terrifying a terrifying statistic – 49% of the adult population in the US is pre-diabetic or living with Type 2, according to the American Diabetes Association.

My doctor gave me a range of where my blood sugar readings should be when I wake up, after eating, and before bed. The analyst part of my brain needed data – so I would eat something, wait a bit, then check my blood sugar. Rinse and repeat. I did this until I identified foods that were delicious and kept my sugar levels in the safe zone. I also learned that there are four factors that affect your blood sugar; food, exercise, medications, and stress.

I'm a gold-star earning student, and I was going to be the best damn diabetes patient this hospital had ever seen, so I took to the first three right away, doctor's orders.

First up, food. I took a good hard look at the food I was eating and cleaned out our house. Everything that I knew would elevate my blood sugar got tossed. We stocked the fridge and pantry with things I knew I could eat. I had been eating like a 12-year-old boy leading up to my diagnosis, so Barry took one for the team and finished the frozen pizzas and Ben & Jerry's, while I replaced them with more vegetables. Leading up to my diagnosis, it was normal for me to drink a bottle of wine to myself every night, if not more. After my diagnosis I stopped drinking - if I wanted to manage this disease effectively and aggressively, drinking my calories was a surefire way to sabotage the mission, so I quit altogether.

Second, exercise. There was a canyon leading up to our street, and I started walking to that canyon every morning. At first, it took about 45 minutes to get from our front door, out to the canyon, down one side, up the other, and then turn around and come home. We purchased some TRX straps and turned the tree in the backyard into a bodyweight gym. I picked a few exercises from the poster that came with the straps and created a workout routine to do when I got done with my morning walk.

Third, medications. I started taking Metformin as prescribed. Prior to my diagnosis, I wasn't on any medications. After my diagnosis, I was taking Metformin twice daily, and the doctor wanted to add a prescription to correct my cholesterol levels as well. I wanted to try and correct the cholesterol naturally through diet and exercise, since I made major lifestyle changes following my diagnosis. I remember feeling scared to advocate for myself, to suggest the diet and exercise route before adding another medication to my routine. We have a choice when the doctor tells us what to do. I'm glad I spoke up, and I'm glad she agreed.

That quadrant - the four factors that affect your blood sugar - became my whole life. When I woke up in the morning, if my blood sugar levels were higher than the range specified by my doctor, I would scan the four areas. What did I eat yesterday? Did I move my body? Did I take my medications as prescribed? How's my stress?

My physical body started seeing results, as one can expect after making dramatic lifestyle changes. Between my diagnosis date and mid-November, I had lost around 15 pounds. However, my blood sugar levels were still elevated. I had my nutrition dialed in, I was walking every morning, and I was taking my medications at the same time every single day. That last section of the quadrant - stress - was what I needed to address. So, I dug deeper and did a scan of the different elements of my life:

Friends? Super solid, feeling very supported.

Marriage? My husband is a saint and is making these lifestyle changes right by my side, he's all in on helping me manage my diabetes.

Work? Ding ding ding.

At the time I was diagnosed, I was working with the marketing firm I had worked with before I left corporate America to skydive full-time. In my role as Director at this firm, I was leading email marketing efforts for NBC, and my diagnosis came the week before fall premieres - easily one of the most stressful times of my career.

I knew I needed to make some changes in my professional life if I wanted to manage this disease effectively. While I had everything else dialed in, the one thing that remained was the stress - I had to get to the root of what was stressing me out.

I worked remotely from our house in San Diego, but I was staffed out of the San Francisco office. It was common for me to fly to SF in the morning and fly home that evening. Every week, I took the train up to LA and spent at least two days in the NBC offices, if not more. This travel was stressing me out, so I made the case to stop traveling. I prioritized doctor's appointments instead of working them around my career. Reducing my travel schedule helped with the stress, but it wasn't enough.

Working in an agency setting, you're on client time. If they need you, they need you. For over a decade, I had been prioritizing client needs over my own. Something had to give.

On the side, I was helping my friend with the branding and marketing for her startup. I knew joining a startup wasn't going to reduce my stress, but I figured if the work I was doing was something I cared about - in this case, women's empowerment and social justice - perhaps I could reduce my stress after all. I started toying with the idea of leaving the agency to join her team, and suggested to my friend that, when she was ready to make her first hire, I was interested in talking about what that could look like. I didn't know if that was actually on her radar, but you never know until you ask.

There were a lot of factors to consider in that kind of a decision, as well. I knew my friend couldn't pay me what I was earning at the agency. I knew she couldn't offer benefits that would compete with unlimited vacation time and platinum-level health care.

NBC wasn't the only work I was doing, and as more got added to my plate, as my stress increased at the agency, I started to seriously consider other options. There are a handful of people I turn to when I'm making big life decisions like this - Barry, of course, as these decisions directly affect him and our quality of life. My mentor Aaron, who has been helping me navigate my career and life since we met at the SXSW Interactive conference in 2009. My best friend Kat, who knows me better than I know myself most of the time. And of course, my family.

When I flew my family to San Diego that Thanksgiving, I had several motives. First and foremost, my dad's birthday periodically falls on Thanksgiving, and in 2017, that was the case. I wanted to do something nice for him. Secondly, my sister and her boyfriend were also coming, and they were surprising Dad for his birthday. Third, my family hadn't seen where I lived since I moved out of their house in 2007. They didn't come visit in Chicago or Austin, or when Barry and I moved back to Chicago, or any of the places we lived in Southern California since moving there in 2011. I wanted them to see how we were living our lives. And to fly four people out to California from Florida was a very *adulty* thing to do, I thought. I wanted them to be proud of the life I had built for myself. Given all the changes that were happening in my life as it related to managing my diabetes, I also wanted to get their opinion on the startup thing.

However, the biggest motivator was rooted more in my desire to save the day. On Thanksgiving the year before, my sister and mom found my dad basically unresponsive on the floor. It was traumatic for both of them and I wanted to provide an opportunity away from their home to create some new holiday memories. I wanted to save everyone. I wanted to be the hero that got the train back on the tracks. For all of my life I had been performing the role of Best Daughter and this was an opportunity to really shine.

The week my folks were in town was magical and my whole family fell in love with San Diego. By the time the actual holiday rolled around, it was showtime. Thanksgiving was Dad's show, and this year, we told him to kick up his feet and relax. It was brilliant. The food was spectacular, dad was impressed, and most importantly, we were able to spend some serious quality time together. After we ate, Dad pulled everyone into the living room.

What followed was an impassioned speech about how each one of us can make a difference and change the world. He gave all of us a sparkly star and talked about the importance of kindness, going for our dreams, and how we can make a mark on the world. My takeaway from the whole thing was this: I have the power to create immense change in the world - starting with me. If I can make changes for myself, then I can impact my community, and when the community is impacted, they start to make changes for themselves and the ripple effect is massive and potent and powerful.

Basically, every wish came true, and then some. My dad had a great birthday, and our all-day Thanksgiving feast was a delicious success. My family got to see where I lived and, not only did they love it, but they wanted to move to San Diego. I had shared what kind of numbers the startup was putting up in its first year to preface why it was a good idea and that this business was on track to start making millions of dollars, and soft-sounded the idea of me leaving the agency to join the team. My parents were enamored by the prospect of me becoming a millionaire and buying property on Sunset Cliffs Boulevard with a little casita in the back for them to call home. Memories were made, life was good. And by the end of the trip, my sister and her boyfriend decided they wanted to get married. On New Year's Eve.

Between Thanksgiving and when we flew to Florida for my sister's wedding for New Year's Eve, I lost another 10 pounds. This chunk of weight loss didn't make sense to me, though. The first 15 pounds I can attribute to the lifestyle changes. But after Thanksgiving, I had a hard time getting motivated to get outside for my daily walks. The food I eat was changing, as it tends to do during the holiday season. I was still taking my medications as prescribed. And though my blood sugar levels were trending down, they were still elevated.

It wasn't until I got home from my sister's wedding and lost another 10 pounds that I started to connect the dots.

Barry and I had flown to Orlando for my sister's wedding, and we were staying with my parents. When we got to their apartment, I sat down on the big chair in the living room - big enough for two people to sit in it - and clarity hit me like a ton of bricks. For most of my life, I had been trying to prove that I wasn't a bad person, that I wasn't a bitch, that I wasn't stupid, and that I wasn't fat. Sitting on that chair, being swallowed by worn brown leather and wrapped up in Barry's arms, I sobbed. The things I was trying to prove I *wasn't* were directly tied to some of the things my sister said to me while I was growing up. Kids being kids, sisters being sisters, and young girls generally being horrible to each other, I wanted to believe my sister didn't mean any of it, and that she was using weaponized language to get what she wanted in those situations. And for whatever reason, I wasn't equipped to know that these things she would say to me were untrue, so I internalized them as truth and then set out on a mission to prove her wrong.

At that point in time I had lost almost 30 pounds since my diagnosis, and sitting on that chair, wrapped in my husband's arms, I felt like I had just lost 100 more. A literal lifetime of feeling like I was a fat, dumb bitch was released. And it felt glorious.

CHAPTER 8

ON THE COUCH, WATCHING THE BACHELOR

hen we got home from my sister's wedding, I jumped right back into work. The first two weeks of January felt like two years. Every day dragged on forever. I was in back-to-back meetings for eight hours a day, and barely had time to get my work done between calls, let alone eat, drink water, and take care of myself. I started having panic attacks. I couldn't peel myself away long enough to rest and recover. Now, not only was I managing NBC's email marketing, I was also the lead on a national commercial campaign. My stress was through the roof. There was one saving grace, however, a little pocket of inspiration.

Between Thanksgiving and my sister's wedding, on my weekly train ride up to LA to work in the NBC offices, I shared a photo on Instagram, outlining my experience managing Diabetes so far. It was the first time I posted about the disease publicly, and within days of posting that photo, I was on the phone with a director and producer from a medical media company. They wanted to follow me and Barry around for a few days and shoot a multimedia documentary about my life since being diagnosed with Diabetes.

In the times I had off during my sister's wedding, I also realized that for my entire career, I had been teaching people how to numb. When I was managing email marketing for NBC, I wanted you to sit on the couch and binge-watch TV shows. When I was launching a new wine brand, I wanted to you to drink lots of wine. When I was writing hilarious hot dog puns as the Wienermobile on Twitter, I wanted you to eat lots and lots of hot dogs. And when I taught David Arquette how to tweet from a plexiglass box on top of Madison Square Garden, I was slinging Snickers candy bars. Everything I thought was a bragging point on my resume wasn't worth bragging about after all. I was a byproduct of the work I had been doing – sick, numb, tired. Something had to change.

Fortunately, my friend with the startup had run the numbers and said she was in a position to make her first hire. Between the agency being so stressful and watching my daily blood sugar readings continue to rise, I made the call. I accepted the offer to join the startup as Chief Marketing Officer, and I would start in February.

The diabetes documentary shoot was scheduled for January 19. I wanted this shoot to be the beginning of the rest of my life. New job, new outlook, a clean slate. On January 18, I called my mentor, Aaron, who was the CMO at the agency I was leaving. I didn't report to him directly, but he played a key role in re-introducing me to corporate America when I retired from skydiving, and I wanted to share the news with him first.

He was appreciative that he was the first call, and of course wished me the best of luck on my new adventure. After I explained my role and the opportunity I was accepting, he walked me through who needed to be notified next, and how to go about doing that. I was a bit emotional during this call, as Aaron had been my first call for so many important professional milestones in my life. I expressed my gratitude for his continued support and hung up the phone.

I felt like I had lost another 100 pounds. I felt free. Immediately after that call, everything felt lighter. The commercial campaign didn't feel like life or death, because I had chosen life.

Later that evening, Barry and I had dinner with the production crew for the documentary.

As we sat down at our booth at Juniper and Ivy with the director, producer, and photographer, I shared the story of how just a few months prior, I was crying over the menu at this restaurant, unsure of what the future would hold for me. In some classic "get to know you" questions, the photographer asked me what I do for work. I shared that I had quit my job earlier that day to pursue a new role. The words Chief Marketing Officer rolled off my tongue and I felt so satisfied with myself. I had set an internal goal for myself to be CMO by the time I was 35, and here I had just accepted a role with that title at 32. I savored that self-congratulatory feeling for all it was worth. After so many years of trauma and pain, it felt good to feel good again.

As dinner carried on, I knew we were in for a treat for this shoot. These folks were not sleazy production types looking to sling products that nobody needs. They were storytellers. Dot connectors. I knew I was in very good hands for this journey.

On the morning of the first day of the shoot, I was showering, listening to my usual playlist, when a song came on that I didn't recognize. In fact, for the first two-thirds of the song, it didn't even register with me. One lyric jumped out, and it was a voice I recognized, Kyle from Slightly Stoopid, a local reggae band. I was a self-diagnosed super fan of Slightly Stoopid and I was amazed that I hadn't heard this song before.

The lyric?

"The choice is yours, the choice is mine, you can't please everybody all of the time."

The song was "Choice is Yours" by a band called Stick Figure. After hearing those words in the shower, it clicked for me. I had been living a life trying to please everyone - my family, my colleagues, my husband, my friends - and it wasn't until the day before hearing this song that I had chosen me. Sure, I had bouts of choosing things for myself here and there, but overwhelmingly, I was living my life for someone else.

I had checked all the boxes - I went to college, I got my degree, I had a good job, I was making lots of money. But I wasn't happy, and I certainly wasn't healthy. It also hit me like a ton of bricks that it was my choices - good, bad, or indifferent - that got me here. Here, literally in this shower in our gorgeous bungalow in San Diego, 32 years old, having just quit a super cushy corporate marketing job to join my friend's startup as a newly diagnosed Diabetic.

The choice was mine. Diabetes empowered me to see that and truly understand it. As I became aware of the fact that I had a choice in every-thing I do - and as I made different choices - my life started to improve dramatically.

The goal for the first day of this shoot was to get the interview por-tion done. As the trucks full of production equipment pulled up to the house, we ushered the lighting and sound guys, along with all their equipment, into the house. Our home had just turned into the set for the documentary. While they were setting up the room for my interview, the photographer and I went down the street to get some stills while the morning light was still soft.

I had never done a photoshoot before, and it was brutally apparent. I was so awkward. Any expectations I had for a photoshoot was rooted in what I saw on TV or in movies. Of course, I had been part of shoots over the course of my career for commercial projects, but it was quite different being on the other side of the camera. I didn't know what to do with my face. I didn't know where to look. I didn't know what to do with my body or how to pose. Tom, my photographer, was kind, patient and, fortunately, insanely talented at his craft, because at each location it would only take a few clicks of the camera to get what he wanted. I had envisioned fans blowing my hair like Beyoncé, cameras clicking hundreds of times to get the shot, being produced and told to channel my inner lion or tiger, and to flash my best Blue Steel. None of that happened. I just walked around the neighborhood, and when Tom saw the shot, he took it. Easy peasy.

Over the course of the rest of the shoot, I felt so alive. After we wrapped on the interview, we collected B-roll. Shots of me sitting on the rocks looking pensive, of Barry and I riding bikes around Coronado Island, paddleboarding at sunrise, cooking at home... and all of it was magical. The most impactful part of the whole journey, however, was seeing Barry's interview portion.

I have known since the day I met Barry that we have a special bond. I truly believe that we have been together for multiple lifetimes, and in each new iteration of my soul, I manage to find him. There is no other way I can wrap my head around the depth of the connection we share.

Still, I'm human and I have baggage. To hear him speak about what it was like to witness me managing this disease - taking this mountain that is Diabetes and breaking it into baby steps - was so powerful. To hear him tell the camera how much he loves me, how much he believes in me, and how he can't wait to see where I go from here, was further confirmation that our connection is as strong as I knew it to be. And, in the midst of hearing these words, I was reminded of the last time I felt so validated, so seen, so supported.

Just a few months earlier, I shared something with Barry that I hadn't shared with anyone else. We were on the couch, watching the Bachelor. Judge me if you want, but I've learned a lot about what NOT to do in relationships by watching that garbage show.

On the episode we were watching, the women were huddled up on a couch in the mansion. One of the contestants said something about an incident that happened to them, and that they never really talk about it with anyone because they're afraid of what people will think of them. Barry paused the show and turned to me:

"Do you worry about that?" Barry asked me.

"Worry about what?"

"Do you not talk about things that happened to you because you're afraid of what people will think about you because it happened to you?" Barry asked.

"Oh yeah, lots of stuff," I replied

Like how I was raped 11 years ago, I thought to myself.

"I just can't believe how women are conditioned to not talk about things that HAPPENED TO THEM. Things that are out of their control. I could never judge a woman for something that happened to her," Barry responded.

I realized in that moment I hadn't felt safe enough to share that story with anyone. I was in my twenties when it happened, and on my couch some 11 years later, I truly felt the weight of the secret I had been carrying by myself for all that time.

At that point, I had been with Barry for seven years and I hadn't told him anything about it. Not because I didn't trust him, but because I buried that part of my life for so long. I swore I would take it to the grave. When we met, I had been having wonderful, healthy sex and figured if the act of sex itself didn't trigger me, then I definitely worked through all the trauma from the rape. And god knows I didn't want to scare this man away with my baggage.

I didn't say anything that night, but my wheels were turning.

Why didn't I tell anyone?

I was a collector as a kid. It started with crystals and rocks and evolved to Backstreet Boys memorabilia and posters (all over my walls of my room growing up), pogs, and Beanie Babies. I would save up my allowance from working with my father to buy the latest release and spent many hours in line in front of the local Hallmark store, as they were our local Beanie Baby dealer.

I had a flashback to when I was a kid. I was in my childhood bedroom, playing with my Beanie Babies. I had quite the collection and had recently built a village for my Beanie Babies out of old boxes, the latest iteration including an elevator made out of an old Jones Soda six-pack container. One of the perks of the newspaper business were the sample bags we'd get from various brands throughout the year. When different companies wanted to distribute samples to a large population of people, they'd provide newspaper carriers with bags containing the samples. These bags were always of inferior quality to the heavy-duty bags we usually used for Sunday papers, which meant we had a lot of samples on the floor of the van by the end of the night.

On the latest sample run, each newspaper bag had an individually boxed bar of Irish Spring soap in it. Combining sharp cardboard corners with flimsy plastic bags was a recipe for sample disaster, and we had soap for years after that particular Sunday.

My Beanie Baby village was almost complete, we just needed a place for the animals to eat. Knowing we had an abundance of small boxes of soap in the garage, I decided to fashion a trough out of a soap box. One of my knockoff Beanie Babies had sprung a leak, and the beans were all over the floor in my bedroom. One way to clean up the mess and recycle the busted beanie was to use the beans as food. Cannibalism wasn't on my radar as a kid, so this seemed like a logical solution.

I made my way down to the garage, grabbed a box of soap, and made my way outside to the van so I could get a boxcutter to open up the box to create the trough. As I held the box of soap in my left hand, I used the box cutter to remove one of the larger panels from the front of the box, leaving a wide, shallow trough where the animals in Beanie Baby Village could all congregate and feed. As I was cutting the final side, the knife slipped and sliced my palm open, about an inch long and deep enough to draw blood, but not require stitches. While I was trying to keep my hand from bleeding profusely, I made my sister swear to secrecy. I knew if she told on me, or if I went to get help for my hand getting cut, I'd get yelled at for being in the van without asking, and I'd get yelled at for using the boxcutter and cutting myself. So, I applied pressure until the bleeding stopped and then grabbed some hydrogen peroxide, Neosporin, and a bunch of band-aids and dressed my wound.

Back in the present moment, I thought to myself; *Wow, I knew at a very young age I'd get yelled at for sustaining this injury, of course I didn't feel safe telling my parents about my rape.*

Over the next few weeks, I'd remember bits and pieces, understanding why I didn't tell anyone.

I had been drinking the night before, and my friend insisted I stay at her place instead of driving home.

I woke up the following morning with my rapist on top of me, a colleague from work.

I took the longest shower of my life when I got home.

Did what I had to do to get Plan B so I wouldn't get pregnant.

And committed to a lifetime of silence.

Girls like me don't get raped.

Work was a toxic battlefield. Every time I went into the kitchen, he was there, leering at me. I freaked out on multiple people, was short with customers, and I found myself acting out in a state of trauma, unwilling and unable to articulate what happened to me.

If I told my manager, would he believe me? Would I get fired? This was my job. Who would believe me? If I couldn't tell my parents, who could I tell? Who would be there for me? Who could I trust?

A few weeks later, Barry and I were sitting on the couch again.

"Remember when you asked if women don't share stuff because they're afraid of being judged for what happened to them?" I asked him, testing the waters.

"Yes," he said.

"Can we talk about something?"

"Of course," he said as he turned off the TV.

I took a deep breath and told him what happened to me. He held me close as I cried, recalling the details of the most violent thing that had happened to my body, mind, and spirit.

I have never longed for a deeper connection with Barry. I have always felt like we were on the same page, even when this was still my deepest darkest secret. But now that I had finally shared this, I felt free from the weight of it. I had been carrying this trauma silently for more than a decade. I didn't realize what a toll this had taken on my body until I felt the weight release after the words escaped my lips. I had sworn to myself I would die with this secret buried within me, and in this moment, to finally let someone else in, to break down the last wall that I had built up, felt nothing short of revolutionary.

To say that my husband is the most supportive man on the planet is the understatement of the century. As I continued watching clips of his interview portion, I was reminded of how lucky I was to share my life with someone like Barry.

We've been through some heavy times since we met. It's never been anything between us, but an onslaught of life events that have happened to us as individuals or around us. This is the stuff that, if you aren't committed to growth, or if you're afraid of change, could completely derail a relationship.

Every time something tragic happened, Barry held me through it. After I retired from skydiving, I struggled to find stable ground. I started to dive deep into personal development to try to find out who I was and what I actually cared about. When Barry lost his job in 2015, effectively ending his skydiving career, a calling he had been tending to for more than 16 years, the transition was gut-wrenching.

Watching the man who taught me how to save my own life have his passion ripped out from under him was brutal, and the months that followed could have killed our relationship, or perhaps even ended our lives. As his time away from the sport got longer, we were drinking more to numb the pain. We both gained 30-40 pounds in the two years that followed our departure from the sport.

That fall, I stumbled into a business relationship with a woman that nearly shattered any shred of confidence I had left. Barry held me through it. After I pulled myself out of that hole, I got honest about what I wanted in my life and near the end of 2015, I accepted a contract with the agency I had been working with before I started skydiving full-time and I told Barry to take as much time as he needed to figure out what he wanted to do next.

Any of these things could have been the end for us. I had seen the demise of previous relationships over things that weren't nearly as serious, so it took a lot of faith on my part to know that this was not like those relationships.

At the end of the day, each instance that could have ruined us brought us closer together. We figured it out. We always do.

In watching his interview and chatting with the production crew, we discussed how relationship dynamics can change in the face of shocking news. Lifestyle changes can be taxing on a relationship if one of the partners has no desire to change. While I was the one with Diabetes, Barry was all in helping me manage the disease, and he didn't stop there. The fact that Barry was right by my side, applying the changes I was making for my health to *his* life was powerful. I didn't have to worry about different grocery lists, I didn't have to worry about temptation in the fridge or pantry - he was all the way on board. He stopped drinking alcohol when I chose to cut it from my life. He held me accountable. He joined me for the bodyweight exercises in the backyard. We started paddleboarding more frequently. He cheered me on as I continued to lose weight, and he supported me leaving the agency and the six-figure salary that provided for our family in order to prioritize my health. He was all in, which made it much easier for me to be all in.

Having the opportunity to share my story with the team from the media company, in this format, was one of the most powerful experiences of my life. I was able to reclaim parts of my story that I had shied away from - particularly my athletic career. To see Barry's love reflected back to me in this way was potent and affirming. As we made our way to the last location on the final day of filming, I started to visualize what this next chapter of my life would look like.

Our last location was Sunset Cliffs for a sunset shoot. I put on my new jeans and a purple sweater, the same shade of purple that was part of the brand colors for the startup I was joining, and I power posed all over Sunset Cliffs. I envisioned these images gracing magazine covers. The main reason I set the goal of being CMO by 35 was so I could grace *40 Under 40* lists, and announcements for *CMO of the Year*. I knew joining this startup was a good choice. I knew I could make a difference there. To know that Barry was behind me 100% made me even more excited for the transition.

After the shoot, my last two weeks at the agency flew by. Before I knew it, Barry was dropping me off at WeWork in downtown San Diego for my first day on the job as Chief Marketing Officer at the startup. I knew I was in for a wild ride by joining an early stage startup, but there is no way I could have predicted what would happen when I got there.

CHAPTER 9

THE BEGINNING
OF THE END

After Barry dropped me off downtown, I went to Starbucks across the street. Usually, when I go to Starbucks, they get my name wrong. Nine times out of ten, I get my cup and it says Cindy on it. On this day, they got my name right.

A sign of good things to come, I thought to myself.

I sat outside of the building at a table and enjoyed my latte and breakfast wrap.

The first day of the rest of my life, I thought. I opened up my banking app and took a screenshot of my bank balance. My business partner told me that we were on track to hit $1M in revenue this year. While I knew that wouldn't automatically make me a millionaire, I wanted to remember what life was like before I made my first million dollars, whenever that was.

The CEO of the startup, Molly, texted to let me know that she would be there shortly, she was looking for parking.

I had connected with her in an online program for female entrepreneurs. The women participating were from all over the country, and Molly was in San Diego. Our career paths were remarkably similar, went to college, did internships, started working in PR. She started her career in DC, I started mine in Chicago. She was working at a boutique agency in San Diego when we went through this program, and I had just started my skydiving event business, Planet Green Socks. We connected immediately, as she was also a spitfire who didn't pull any punches when it came to voicing her opinions. With blonde hair and piercing blue eyes, combined with her firecracker personality, Molly turned heads everywhere she went.

We had been chatting online and participating in the group calls for the program for nearly six months before we finally met in person. A bunch of the women who went through the program were gathering for an in-person retreat, and the venue was a quick 15-minute drive from where I lived. I was so excited to meet these women, Molly in particular.

That retreat was a whirlwind, but I knew she and I would stay connected after the event. We were seated next to each other during one of the retreat sessions, taking notes, making light of all the flowery woo-woo language the speakers were using. It felt so fake and forced, we both just rolled our eyes and laughed. This retreat occurred on the one-year anniversary of Adam's death. I was so fed up with the presenter on this particular session, I almost walked out in the middle of it, but I stuck it out. After she was done talking, I went out to the garden to sit under the trees. I needed some space.

The following session was about marketing, so I passed. I didn't need someone to tell me the basics of how to build a website or why you should definitely always try to be building your email list. Instead of sitting through another session full of information I already knew, I spent my time under the trees, thinking about Adam. As if on cue, the winds kicked up and swirled around me. The whole experience was overwhelming, it felt like Adam was sitting on the bench next to me. I started this online program after my first event for my company, and the last event I coordinated was Adam's memorial. After we released his ashes above the skies at the drop zone we were training at with our respective teams, I had zero desire to be involved in skydiving ever again. I knew I wouldn't jump again, and if I had my way about it, I'd never set foot on another drop zone.

After I collected my thoughts and wiped the tears from my eyes, I made my way back upstairs to the room I was staying in. Not long after I laid down on the bed, Molly came in.

"You would not believe the bullshit they're talking about down there," she said.

She turned on her valley girl voice.

"Did you know, that, like, you should totally have your opt-in happen above the fold on your website because, like, that's where people can see it?" she said, mocking the speaker.

It was exactly what I needed to take my mind off of Adam.

She sat down on the bed and asked me how I was doing. She knew that this was Adam's anniversary. I told her about my experience under the trees, how I started this program wanting to build out this company and tour the USA hosting badass events, and how, since Adam's memorial event, I hadn't really felt the fire for anything, really.

"You know, if you kill Planet Green Socks, you aren't killing Adam. He's already dead," Molly said.

It felt like another release. Who was this beautiful angel? How did she know exactly what I needed to hear? How did she know that I was ready to be all the way done with Planet Green Socks, but was feeling shame around the decision?

I started crying again. She held me and told me everything would be okay. I believed her.

Back in front of WeWork, I stood up excitedly to greet Molly. I showed her my Starbucks cup, laughing about how they got my name right, so today was the best day, and we hadn't even begun to save the world together yet. I felt warm all over. I finally made it. She was one of the cool kids, and she liked me enough to be friends *and* to hire me. My middle school self was stoked.

We made our way upstairs, got a quick rundown of everything that was available to us as members of this coworking space, and received our welcome materials. Behind us was a kitchen complete with Kombucha on tap. We filled up our cups and made our way to the lobby to catch an elevator. The lighting in the lobby was bright purple and we joked about how even the lighting was on-brand for us here. As we wandered through the different floors and explored the office space that was available, we talked about expansion plans, and how WeWork could definitely accommodate any growth, at least for the first few years.

We arrived on the highest floor available to us, picked out a booth, dropped off our stuff, and took a lap around the floor. There were corner offices available, some with views of the bay. When I was in my first agency job, I remember telling a friend that within ten years, I'd be running my own team in an office in San Diego with views of the bay. I didn't know why I said San Diego, I had never even visited the city. I hadn't even gone skydiving yet, so my path to get out to California was unclear. When I said that, I surprised myself, because it sounded so outlandish for an entry-level agency employee to be spouting off about leading teams, let alone doing so on the other side of the country in a city she'd never been to.

"Holy shit, I made it. Maybe I'm psychic," I thought to myself as we made our way back to the common area where we had dropped off our stuff.

There was no real orientation necessary here, I had been helping Molly with her marketing and branding off and on for the year leading up to accepting the offer to join the team full-time. Our first order of business was to launch our seed round of venture capital fundraising. This was my first task – raise one million dollars.

I had never done venture fundraising before, but I did all the research I possibly could. The cool thing about how we were launching this round was that we were doing it with a platform called SeedInvest. The fact that Molly had been accepted into the platform was one of the reasons I was keen to join the team so early. This platform allowed everyday folks to invest in the company, not just established investors. We could offer our friends and family the opportunity to invest in the company, Shark Tank style, without spending Shark Tank money. Neither one of us came from money, so to be able to bring this opportunity to our communities was intoxicating. I felt like Lisa Kudrow in *Romy and Michelle's High School Reunion* where she starts talking about how she's a very serious businesswoman.

And since our friends and family weren't rolling it (yet), we were pleased to know that SeedInvest had a network of tons of investors that we'd have access to on the platform. They had a checklist for us to help us navigate what we should do to get the word out about the round and what we should do to execute the round itself.

I came armed and ready with a marketing plan that would let folks know what we were up to – a fully integrated program that spanned across email, social media, friends and family, press outreach, and a few tricks up my sleeve that I was excited to share with her.

The plan was to launch this round as soon as we could, and we needed to raise at least $175,000 to keep what we raise, otherwise it would be returned to the investors at the end of the campaign. We submitted all of our plans and paperwork for approval and the marketing plan was approved, but they needed more information on revenue, statistics and projections. We finally got all of our ducks in a row a few weeks later, and we were scheduled to start fundraising on International Women's Day. Given that our company was a skincare line that was also all about empowering women and social justice, it felt like fate. I genuinely believed we were ready to go.

As we discussed where everything was going and who was responsible for what, it was blatantly obvious to me that it was going to be a while before I got to the marketing part of my job. I was a full-time fundraiser, production assistant, supply chain manager, errand runner, CEO supporter, and then at the bottom of the list of the hats I'd be wearing was why I was actually there: to market this product and make sure as many people get it as possible. I knew I'd be responsible for a lot of tasks outside of marketing, but this was feeling more like a co-founder role to me. It felt risky to ask for what I wanted so early in our working relationship, but I'd never know unless I tried.

I told Molly that I was super excited to be here, and I had no problem wearing multiple hats, but I needed something more. I wanted to have more skin in the game. I asked if I could be considered a Co-founder and she said yes and that we'd talk about what equity changes and salary changes needed to be made after we got through the fundraising.

When International Women's Day rolled around, it was game time. We made the announcements, sent the emails, posted to social media posts, and got our friends and family rallied up to help us spread the word. In the first few weeks, we raised $75,000. We had support coming in from some of the most unexpected places. My network jumped in with donations ranging from the $500 minimum up to commitments of $25,000. I had never asked my community for anything in the 10+ years I had been cultivating professional and personal relationships, and I was blown away by their support. Knowing that my contacts were helping us inch closer to our goal in such significant ways made me feel like I was contributing to this business in an impactful way, beyond the skills I brought to the table.

When it rains, it pours, and opportunity was raining down on our company like we could have only dreamed about. Shortly after we launched the seed round, we received an order from a national retailer with stores in more than 400 shopping malls in the United States. When Molly got the purchase order, I thought she was going to pass out. When she got another purchase order later that day, we were confused. They had already sent through a PO, was this a separate one or was this an update to the original? The two purchase orders totaled more than $70,000, by far the biggest order we had ever received.

When we got this order, we were doing everything by hand. We purchased bottles from one vendor, labels from another, and labeled all of the products ourselves. We purchased all of the ingredients for the products and made them by hand. We were doing all of this out of her apartment – mostly in the living room, kitchen area, and in the spare bedroom – no more than 500 square feet of working space. We looked at the total number of units ordered. More than 14,000. My eyes must have been the size of dinner plates, I was so shocked and excited and overwhelmed by the news.

When we got a response from the vendor that yes, there were two orders, and yes, the total was correct, time stood still. We looked at each other and squealed. We had a dance party. We told the women who were helping us with production the good news. It was one of the most exciting days of my life.

It was also the beginning of the end.

We were struggling to find the funds necessary to purchase supplies for this order. I hadn't been paid on time yet and I had taken a nearly 50% pay cut to pursue this opportunity, so naturally, I was a bit panicked. I figured if I could help us get the order filled, then I'd have a chance of getting paid. I offered to put the expenses on my personal credit card, as I had accumulated quite a bit of available credit when I was working at the agency. Molly was nervous to accept, and I honestly didn't see any other way. As a business, we didn't have access to resources to get this done, and I was so blinded by the lack of paychecks I was receiving, it was truly the only path I could see that would get me paid and not put me at risk of total financial ruin.

After she agreed to let me fund the first order, we ordered all of the supplies. A cool $11,000 later, our supplies started rolling in. It was time to get to work.

A typical day looked like this: Drop Barry off at work around 7 am, go straight to Molly's apartment and get to work. Depending on the needs of that day, we'd make product, label jars, post on social media, promote the seed round, prepare for upcoming pitches to investors, ship out product for online orders, and try to remember to eat. I was pulling 16-18-hour days, taking as many boxes of product home with me as I could to try to get ahead on the next day's deliverables.

The apartment turned into a pressure cooker as time wore on. As boxes full of product ready to be shipped piled up, there was less space in the apartment. Molly was literally living in her work, and it was starting to take a toll on her.

On the morning she was scheduled to pitch to the largest global network of angel investors, she called me over early. I arrived and she was in the middle of a panic attack, in the fetal position on the couch. Her husband was trying to calm her down, but she wasn't having it. She was crying, screaming, and shaking, I had never seen her like this, and I was concerned for her. I wanted to fix it and make it all go away. When her husband recommended cancelling the call, she wailed even louder. I put my hand on her arm and looked her in the eyes. I knew this was a huge moment for the business, and for her personally. I also knew she wasn't going to pull it together in time, the call was in 30 minutes. The call was a quick 10-minute pitch to confirm the network's interest. If they liked what we had to say, they'd send us on a roadshow to pitch their investor networks around Southern California.

"I've heard you do this pitch a million times, I helped you with the deck, I could do this for you."

She pulled away from me and turned to her husband.

"This is *my* pitch, I don't want her to do it," she wailed, louder than before.

Her husband and I locked eyes and I knew it wasn't going to happen. The call wasn't going to happen. We were going to have to reschedule a call with the very folks who would be able to fund this entire round if they wanted to.

What was the point of saying yes to me being co-founder if she couldn't let me support her in this very dire time of need? I understood how much work she'd done to get the company to this point. Is this what the rest of this business relationship was going to look like? Did she not trust me? Did she not think I could handle it? If it were me, and it came down to rescheduling the call that could very well change the trajectory of this company or allowing my business partner to facilitate the conversation, I would want to make sure the conversation still happened. But this wasn't my company to run.

"Would you like for me to email them and let them know you aren't feeling well and see if they can reschedule?" I asked.

She looked at me and her eyes softened. She nodded yes.

I was seething with rage.

Well, at least she'll let me communicate with them and let them know it's not happening today. I thought to myself, gritting my teeth and rage typing on my keyboard.

For the rest of the day, the image of her pulling away from me when I suggested I take the call kept replaying on a loop in my mind. The look in her eyes was a mix of rage, fear, and disgust. This triggered something deep within me and for the rest of the day, and for every day moving forward, I found myself walking on eggshells around her, afraid she'd break if I said the wrong thing at the wrong time. And frankly, I was afraid I'd break too.

I started having panic attacks after that. I'd usually have at least one per day, some days I'd have two. Things were moving so fast between the fundraising and filling these big orders, it was all I could do to hang on and stay alive. I noticed my blood sugar readings were trending back to levels I hadn't seen since right after my diagnosis. To try to keep myself sane between tasks, I'd take a lap around the apartment complex. Molly and I would have walking meetings to help keep the energy moving, because if I was in that apartment for too long, I got cranky and anxious.

I was walking to get lunch for the team, talking to Barry on the phone, when I started getting dizzy. I told him I needed to hang up because I wanted to have both hands free. I kept walking, trying to take deep breaths as I made my way to the restaurant around the corner. I stood about a block away from the restaurant and started texting Molly to let her know I was having a panic attack and that I needed help. I made my way to the restaurant; told them I was there to pick up food and that I was having a panic attack and that I needed a glass of water. I sat down and my chest felt like an elephant was sitting on it, my heart was racing, and I felt completely disconnected from my body.

A few minutes later, Molly came running into the restaurant. She had sprinted from the apartment, terrified of what she might find. I sat for a bit and collected myself, and then we made our way back to work.

This pattern would continue for the weeks leading up to the shipment of the first order. I would work insane hours, bring product home with me to label late into the night and again in the morning before I got to Molly's apartment, then spend all day there hopping in to help with production between my fundraising and marketing duties. I'd go for a walk, have a panic attack, and be rendered useless for a bit, then power through to finish what I was doing when the panic attack came on.

As if on cue, the Universe dumped another opportunity on us. We were asked to host a sale with one of the largest e-commerce sites in the world. The way it worked was pretty simple: we tell them how much inventory we have, they list it, and when it's gone, the sale is over. We took a look at what we had at the warehouse, gave those numbers to the vendor, and launched the sale.

Our products were flying off the digital shelves for this sale, and our physical inventory was depleted quickly. Not one to miss out on a revenue opportunity, Molly logged into the backend of the e-commerce site and made more inventory available, and then instructed me to order the supplies for the products we'd need to make more of to fill the order.

As I was ordering supplies, I realized none of these items would get here on time without significant fees for expedited shipping. Molly didn't care. The volume was coming in and that was her only focus – sell as many products as possible, strike while the iron is hot, show traction for the investors. I proceeded to rush order supplies and when our usual vendors were out of what we needed, I sought out other options, most of which were more expensive than our usual wholesale vendors. If she said it was okay, I wasn't going to question it. This was her ship, she made that abundantly clear around our fundraising pitch conversation. I was just trying to get things out the door so maybe I could get paid on time.

The e-commerce giant wasn't our only retail customer. As the deadline for our first big order crept up on, we called in all the troops to help us get this order out the door. Barry joined us for a day of adding barcodes to products, and swore he'd never help again after he heard how Molly was talking to me. He said if I wanted to subject myself to that, that was my choice, but in order to continue to support me in this decision, he needed to never be around her ever again. It felt like I just woke up from the deepest slumber of my life. I hadn't even registered that the way we were interacting wasn't healthy. I was so busy I didn't have the capacity to establish boundaries or have challenging conversations.

The order was supposed to be picked up the following morning, and we still had hundreds, if not thousands of products to create before the truck came to pick up the pallet.

On pickup day, a teammate from my improv class came in at 5 a.m. and helped me make bath salts and sugar scrubs. We were in the kitchen, furiously dipping jars into buckets of product, trying to make the most efficient assembly line we could while Molly slept. By 8 a.m., it was abundantly clear that this order was not going out today.

I was livid. I had been killing myself to get these products done, having panic attacks every day, having friends come join me at 5 a.m., having fights with my husband about how Molly was conducting herself in front of her employees, and for what? Facial oil?

Molly called her assistant and asked her to see if we could get the pickup time scheduled for another day. Apparently, we had the dates wrong.

This pallet wasn't being picked up until Monday.

CHAPTER 10

YOU DON'T NEED THE MONEY

My professional rock bottom happened on April 20, 2018.

We were working to get the second pallet ready for the big order, and I was juggling inventory issues at the warehouse for the big e-commerce order. This was the biggest shitshow I had ever been a part of. Molly had authorized more and more inventory for the sale, high on the success of the sale and the traction we were getting. To compensate for the additional inventory we needed to create, we paid a premium for ingredients, containers, and expedited shipping to get it all here on time. We called the warehouse and had them hold all shipments for 10 days while we tried to get caught up on inventory. Every time we sent more items, it wasn't enough. So, we'd repeat the cycle; rush order supplies, rush through production, rush ship to the warehouse. Meanwhile, despite the inventory hold, the warehouse kept filling orders. It was an absolute disaster, and I was quickly running out of patience.

I got a note from the warehouse that our latest inventory resupply was damaged in transit. Nearly all of the product was unusable. It was the perfect storm – our usual vendor for the face wash bottles weren't going to get here on time, despite placing an emergency order. We found an alternative vendor, paid a higher price for the bottles, rush shipped them, filled the bottles with the expensive ingredients we rush ordered, then realized the bottles didn't have locking mechanisms on the pump lid to keep the product from leaking on the way to the warehouse. We had zero options at that point, so we packaged the bottles as best we could, tried to pad it enough to keep the bottles upright, and then overnighted that order, to the tune of $800, to get it to the warehouse on time. It didn't work. They leaked. On top of that, the leaking face wash also stripped most of the other products of their labels, so what wasn't broken wasn't labeled.

Before I closed my computer, I got a Slack message notification.

It was Molly's assistant. Considering the confusion on the pallet dates the first time, I had asked her assistant to get clarity from the national retailer – was the date on the order the date they were sending a truck to pick up the pallet? Was it the day product needed to arrive in the warehouse? Was that an in-store-by date?

The date we shipped the pallet was the day the product was due at their warehouse.

I closed my computer, feeling the sensation of heavy weight on my chest that happens before I have a panic attack. I'd been having them enough to know when it was about to come and how bad it would be, and this was going to be a doozy. On one of the last panic attacks I had, she kept asking me questions. I was having a hard time processing what was happening in my body, and there was no energy to answer questions. The questions made my brain short circuit and exacerbated the panic attack. Due to the prevalence of panic attacks we were having lately, Molly and I had established a communication process – if I was aware of what was happening and could remove myself from the environment I was in to try to get ahead of it and calm myself, I would do that. So, the plan was to ask for help if you're capable and able to receive, otherwise, get out and take care of yourself, and the other person will let you do that.

At this point, we were in the final days of production for the second order for the national retailer and scrambling to figure out how to fix the inventory issue for the big e-commerce order. We had five people in the apartment helping with production, plus me, Molly, her husband popping in and out, and their two dogs. The living room had a very narrow passageway between stacks of finished product, there were buckets of ingredients in stations between the walkways; a table set up by the couch, kitchen table, over the stove, over the sink, in the guest bathroom, a table and chairs on the patio, and two more stations in the guest room which was serving as our office and partial production facility. The apartment was a pressure cooker with so many humans working such long hours in such confined spaces.

I grabbed my computer and said I'd be back in a bit.

Molly glared at me. She didn't know I was on the verge of losing it.

"I'm about to have a panic attack and I need to remove myself from this apartment," I said, recalling the communication process we'd established for this exact scenario.

She looked at me, disgusted, as if my incoming panic attack was a personal slight against her.

I felt the panic attack coming, but the look she gave me made me pause. I needed to wrap things up here. I started stammering, one of my first symptoms other than the elephant-on-chest feeling, updating the teammates on what the status was at the station I had been working. I tried to organize the materials that were on the table to set it up for the next person. I was embarrassed that this was happening, which made me frustrated. When I wasn't able to communicate clearly, I felt ashamed, and everyone else could feel it.

"Get out of here," she hissed.

"I literally just said that's what I'm doing, Molly, just let me collect my things."

I could feel her eyes on me, burning into my back as I navigated around and over piles of product. I could feel her frustration building, and she may as well have been tapping her toe.

"What's your deal?" she pressed.

I took a deep breath. We had just discussed how we would navigate a situation like this and pressing the way she just did was not part of the plan. I succumbed to my frustration and rage and felt the trauma tornado take over.

"I'M A TYPE 2 DIABETIC ON THE VERGE OF FINANCIAL RUIN, MOLLY."

There it was. Every fear I had about this job and my ability to handle it was out there on the table, for every person who was in this room to witness.

I explained that my blood sugar was on the rise, that I was overwhelmed, that I had extended nearly all of my personal credit for these orders and I still hadn't been reimbursed or paid a paycheck, and on top of all of that, these orders we've been slaving over are either damaged or late. I was alarmed by how quickly everything was melting down, and how little concern there seemed to be for this on her end.

I also said I wouldn't be funding anything else for this company.

The look in her eyes was one I had seen before, a mix of rage, disgust, impatience, and a general air of "you're a problem that needs to be fixed."

I had seen this look in my dad's eyes growing up, and that sent me on another spiral, feeling like a little girl getting scolded.

I left shortly after that, feeling physically hot with rage.

Was that the best way for me to advocate for myself? Probably not. But I had never actually articulated my fears or my needs in such a way, and even though it wasn't graceful - I felt proud of myself. I knew my panic attacks well enough to know when they were coming, I knew how my brain gets scrambled during a panic attack, and was able to create a communication process that would hopefully alleviate the additional stress I put on myself when I feel shame for not being able to communicate clearly.

This was such a jump from the panic attacks I had when I worked at the agency. Those panic attacks felt like they came out of nowhere, because I didn't know the signs. And the surprise of the attack plus the energy drain from the attack itself would wipe me out for an entire day, if not two days. While I'd rather not have so many panic attacks that I can clearly identify the symptoms, I was thankful for that level of awareness.

But this amount of anxiety wasn't healthy, normal, or sustainable. I needed a reset button. I remembered I still had some unfinished business with the Trans-Catalina Trail, and even if I couldn't walk right for a few weeks after that first hike, I knew it would help me clear my head. Barry and I had promised each other that we would do the whole trail again someday and I wanted someday to be tomorrow.

I looked at the calendar and I figured we could do our second attempt at the TCT for my 33rd birthday during the first week of June. At that point, the big orders would have shipped, and the dust would have settled, and it would be a good time for me to take a break to walk across the island and hit the reset button. After my reaction earlier, it was abundantly clear that I needed some nature therapy. Worst-case scenario, my trauma tornado would get me fired and I probably wouldn't even be with the company come June, so there would be nothing in my way of fully experiencing whatever the trail had to offer me this time, without my having to rush back to work.

For the next week, I worked from home, handling office-type work while the team cranked away on production for both orders. Molly was getting ready to go on a road trip around the L.A. area, pitching to different angel investors, and I was managing everything else to give her space to prep. When pitch week came, I started going back to the apartment to keep an eye on production and make sure the orders were coming along swiftly. Not being in the physical production space had done wonders for my sanity, my blood sugar readings were back to normal while I was working from home, *and* they were great during the pitch week, despite the additional workload.

When Molly returned, things got wild again. We ended up cancelling all the orders from the big e-commerce sale because we couldn't fill the orders and were losing money on the deal with all of the inventory issues. We had a list a mile long of our regular customers who were waiting on orders while we were trying to figure out that whole situation. Everything started moving quickly again. I still hadn't been reimbursed for the orders I had funded, and the first two paychecks I received had a hold on them due to insufficient funds in the company bank account. The panic attacks returned.

Fortunately, I had an outlet for all of this. I was enrolled in improv classes at Finest City Improv when all of this was going down, and my classmates became my chosen family. I hadn't found a community like this since I was skydiving, and even though things were stressful for me professionally, my social life was a massive source of inspiration. The class was held on Sunday and that theater became my church. Our class was in the theater itself, not in the classroom, so for the duration of our seven weeks together, we got tons of stage time.

One night the owner of the theater had a Bon Voyage party, as she was leaving San Diego to sail up the east coast for the summer. I met some of my classmates at the theater and settled in for a great show.

Over the course of the evening, I watched as some of the house improv teams, instructors, the owner herself, and folks from the audience got on stage to play. They made up special games, some of the acts were scripted, and in general, it was a hilarious and powerful time. When it came down to the part where everyone shared how the theater owner and this community have impacted their lives, I braced myself. I was overwhelmed with emotion. I hadn't even really met this woman but hearing the impact she made on everyone was so moving. While I was skydiving, I had been to so many memorials, witnessing an outpouring of stories and love and support for the skydivers who had passed away. It was soothing to read in the funeral program, and healing for folks to share these impactful moments in an effort to keep the deceased's spirit alive, but I couldn't help but wonder if the person who passed had any idea the impact they made on their community while they were alive. I constantly wished that we were better at sharing these anecdotes with people while they're on this planet to hear them. This night was exactly that.

My classmate, the same one who came to help make products for the big orders, was sitting next to me during the show and saw me crying. She pulled me aside after the show and asked if she could tell me something.

"Of course you can!"

She dragged me outside and gave it to me straight:

"If you want what you saw tonight, you already have it here. We love you like that. You don't need the job or the money or any of it to be happy. You don't need the money."

I started crying again. This woman only knew Sydney at her full expression. Improv was my safe space to be me, to be extra, to take up space, to explore my creativity, to feel feelings, and to figure out how to express them in different ways. My classmate was often apologizing for her sometimes-broken English since it wasn't her first language. There was nothing broken about this message.

I hugged her and cried, thanking her for seeing me so clearly. It's a blessing to have a place where one can feel completely comfortable being their authentic self, and to be seen in that state is one of the greatest gifts on earth.

After that night, I knew I had dreams bigger than facial oil and I couldn't ignore them anymore. I realized my trigger was being in the presence of someone so fearlessly pursuing their dreams and doing whatever it takes to keep that dream alive. I got so spun up when I saw how Molly went after these big orders because I had been putting my dreams and my health and everything else on the back burner. Once I saw that I couldn't unsee it.

I wanted to make an impact and I wanted to make it in my own way. If my recommendations here were falling on deaf ears, it was time for me to go find my dream and chase it.

Molly had mentioned we needed to have a conversation about what happened on the 20th but kept putting it off. After we canceled the big e-commerce order, I kept working from home, offering to come in to help with production if needed, and she told me she had it under control. When it came time to do the pallet for the second order from the national retailer, I felt like a stranger among the group. The other girls were distant, and Molly was too. Later that week, she said she was ready to have a call about The Event.

At this point, I'd had nearly a month to reflect on what happened, how I reacted, what I'd do differently, and what kind of support I needed moving forward. I realized in my unpacking of the situation that I had been seriously triggered, and my default reactions were ones I had absorbed from my father. I realized that the way I showed up was learned behavior, and I didn't like how I felt when it happened, so I was in the process of unlearning.

As a result, I figured out that when I get stressed, it's hard for me to articulate myself clearly. I thought about what kind of environment would make me feel safe to share and would give me enough time to hear what was said and show up in a way that feels authentic to me. As long as my default reaction was to fly off the handle and overreact, I had to create space for myself to process and feel safe. I also knew that unless I was very specific about what I needed from Molly to facilitate a productive conversation, I'd likely end up in another situation where I get frustrated, feel shame wash over me, and then move straight into a trauma tornado.

I suggested that she says everything she needs to say, and I'd take notes. That way, I don't interrupt. When she was done and she felt like she had gotten everything out, then I would reflect on my notes, ask for clarity where I needed it, and then I can respond from that place. For me to arrive at full understanding of what was happening and respond in the way I want to show up versus my learned reactions, I needed to have all of the information. Then I would do the same – say my part, uninterrupted, answer questions for clarity, receive Molly's response. The way we had been communicating up until this point wasn't working, so maybe this would help.

I felt like it made a big difference. Giving myself the space to listen allowed me to really understand what she was saying, versus hearing it through the filters of my trauma and learned responses. I had the chance to hear it, let it sit, arrive at my own conclusions and respond from that place, versus jumping in and reacting to each thing she said as she said it.

When it came time to talk about the financial side of things, I was firm in my stance. If paying me wasn't going to be a priority, then the funding stopped. I could not simultaneously continue to extend my personal credit to the business while not being paid. I wasn't independently wealthy, and Barry was working a part-time job. I had no savings to speak of. I wouldn't have suggested this arrangement if I had reason to believe I wouldn't get paid or reimbursed.

"When shit gets hard, you run," she said.

She was referencing what happened after I funded the first order. When time kept passing by and the money wasn't coming back to me, I freaked out. I was scared about putting that much credit on the line, but I didn't see any other options. We weren't going to turn down this order - this could put us on the map. Molly already had loans that were deducted from her account daily. Friends and family were tapped. It was a lot of pressure, yet also one of the easiest decisions I've ever made. I believed in this company, and I thought this action demonstrated that. Instead, I was berated for having fears tied to the decision.

"That isn't fair, and you know it," I responded.

She went on to tell me that if I really wanted Co-Founder status, then I should be okay with not getting paid. Everyone else should get paid before the Co-Founder, she said. At this point, Co-Founder was a title to make me feel like I had more skin the game, we hadn't discussed equity changes or what that would look like, as initially promised. Furthermore, it was my credit that was keeping this company open. I was the biggest investor in the company at that point, aside from the money Molly had spent to start the business.

I had asked about division of labor - who was actually in charge of what - and she pivoted the conversation. She started talking about running the numbers and how she actually couldn't afford my salary, despite what she said to get me signed on.

She didn't outright fire me, and I didn't quit, but ultimately, it was my choice - keep working and do it for free because she can't afford me or leave the company.

I slept on it and the next day I called on my Trust Tree - the people who serve as my personal Board of Directors of sorts.

Barry had been right by my side for all of this and he supported whatever choice I wanted to make and didn't want to sway my decision with his opinions. I talked about the whole situation with my best friend Kat. She was in a similar relationship with the owner of the restaurant she was the chef at, and it was helpful to hear how she was handling things on her end.

When I really needed to think, I would drive to Sunset Cliffs in San Diego and park by the water. Sometimes I'd take a walk, sometimes I'd sit on a bench, sometimes I wouldn't even get out of the car. This was my happy place for the shoot, this is where I brought my family when I was getting their feedback on the transition to the startup, this is where I caught sunsets on Adam's birthday and the anniversary of his passing, and this is where I know I can always clear my head. So, I got in the car and went to the cliffs.

I pulled into my usual spot right by a big cove, where sometimes I can feel the waves crashing into the cliffs while sitting in my car. Today was one of those days. Big crashing waves and brilliant sunshine. The perfect San Diego day.

I called Aaron, my longest-standing mentor, and told him the situation. I was a bit exasperated, as just over three months ago, I was calling him to tell him I was leaving the agency for the startup, and now here I was, lamenting about the situation I found myself in. I told him about extending my credit, as well as the cash flow and quality control issues. I told him what my options were.

"I think it's time for you to write the book, Sydney."

I gasped.

"I've been watching how your writing is evolving and you have such a gift. You're ready. Go write it."

I closed my eyes and fought back tears. This guy. Giving me a dose of permission that I couldn't give myself to go do what I've always wanted to do: write a book. He said I had survived so much, and it could help people. I was so thankful to be seen in this way. This wasn't a conversation about how I had only been there for 90-something days and that I should stick it out. This wasn't a judgment about how I make poor career choices. This was an opportunity. An opportunity to choose me, to do something I want to do, and to do it right now. This was my time.

The choice was mine.

I thanked him for his time and said I'd be in touch about the whole book writing thing when I got my head wrapped around what that would look like.

I collected my thoughts, put my seatbelt on, and drove home. I knew what I needed to do.

CHAPTER 11

HIKING MY FEELINGS

After 95 panic attack inducing days at the startup, I quit. No backup plan, no savings to speak of, no other jobs lined up. It was the hardest decision I ever made, and the easiest decision I ever made at the same time.

I had to reckon with how I oversold myself on the opportunity. I had to hold myself accountable for how I was triggered, and how that impacted my ability to think clearly, perform at my best, and show up how I want to show up. I had to give myself permission to release the shame of not knowing what I didn't know. There was no way I could have known what I was walking into. I didn't know what to ask. The questions I knew to ask were answered beautifully. I had to face the "what ifs" – what if I stayed? What if they get a big deal and start making millions or billions of dollars? What if I miss out on that? Is it worth it?

That's when it became the easiest decision. No, it wasn't worth it. No matter how much money we would or wouldn't make, it wasn't worth having panic attacks every day while we figure out how to make ends meet. It wasn't worth my blood sugar levels elevating to numbers I hadn't seen since right after my diagnosis. It wasn't worth the strain on my marriage. It wasn't worth putting myself into more debt. If I was dead, I couldn't enjoy the fruits of my labor, and I wasn't even enjoying the labor part of it. And then there was that whole "find my dream and chase it" bit, too. I couldn't keep killing myself for something that wasn't mine.

So, I quit. I was still waiting to be reimbursed for the last order I funded, so I wasn't able to rip the proverbial bandage completely off, but at least I was out of there. Within a few days, my blood sugar levels settled back down.

I don't know if I'm psychic, if this was a self-fulfilling prophecy, or if it was just a coincidence, but now I had two weeks to train for the Trans-Catalina Trail and no responsibilities to return to when I got done with that adventure.

Four days after I left the startup, Barry and I went for a hike outside of San Diego. I was trying out a pair of trail runners for the first time as opposed to hiking boots and this was the first hike we had done in a while. The first 30 or so minutes were pretty rough - my chest was congested and I just wanted to clear it out, my legs were on fire on the initial climb out of the parking area, and though I had been walking a lot while I was at the startup, those walks were on flat level ground. As we made our way above the tree line, I saw a railing that would help us get to the summit.

One of the reasons we picked this hike was the view from the top, but "May gray" was in full effect. May grey is the marine layer that blankets coastal Southern California in May, which fades into "June gloom" before opening up to warmer weather in July. At the summit, it was completely blocking the views we were looking forward to. I had Barry snap a picture anyway. As I watched the squirrels beg for my almonds, I took stock of everything that had happened so far this year. The documentary, leaving the agency, joining the startup then leaving it, and now here I was, actually training for the Trans-Catalina Trail. At this point, I had lost 60 pounds since my diabetes diagnosis. Considering I had just left two jobs in a span of five months, I was shocked that I didn't feel more stressed. In fact, I wasn't stressed at all. For the first time in a long time, it felt like I could exhale after proverbially holding my breath for months. And at this moment, on this summit, I could let it all out. So, I did.

I thought about the last time I went through something this stressful - the last half of 2014. After Adam died, everything happened so fast, life felt like tragedy after tragedy and all I could do was numb to cope with it. In fact, at this time of my life, I wasn't deploying my normal coping mechanisms. In 2014, I'd jump into a pint of Ben & Jerry's, and I was drinking a bottle of wine to myself almost every night.

So how *was* I coping? Since I was diagnosed with Diabetes, I kicked the ice cream and wine to the curb. I realized was hiking my feelings. And that felt a lot better than eating or drinking my feelings, but it wasn't enough. Something was missing.

Later that week, Barry and I set out to complete the Mission Trails Regional Park 5 Peak Challenge in one day. This would replicate the first day on the Trans-Catalina Trail, and if we could get through this, we could definitely handle the TCT.

One of the things I did before I made the decision to make room for more adventure in my life was take the Clifton Strengths Assessment.

This test is a series of questions designed to help you articulate your strengths and provides a thorough reading of what those traits are and how you may have seen them show up over the course of your life.

I was at a particularly low point, questioning who I am, how I show up, and why I'm here. I had been in a swirling pit of mismanaged expectations (mine and others) and projections (mine and others), and I was having a hard time remembering who the hell I was and what I was good at. So, I took this assessment. The results weren't shocking, but they were everything I needed at the time so I could get back to center, find my confidence, and make some decisions.

While hiking these five peaks, I found myself thinking about these traits and how, for all of my life, I'd been fighting to understand why I react the way I do to certain things, how I work, how I process information, how I approach relationships, all of it.

Not surprisingly, the order in which we completed the peaks follows my strengths, in order:

#1: COWLES MOUNTAIN - EMPATHY

 Empathy: People who are especially talented Empaths can sense the feelings of other people by imagining themselves in others' lives or situations.

Ascending Cowles, I was struggling. It felt like it was taking me way longer than usual to get warmed up. I started to worry about whether or not I was going to be able to make it all day, as this was the first long hike we'd attempted since I was diagnosed with Type 2 Diabetes.

Prior to picking hiking back up, I met with my doctor to talk about any concerns I had while preparing for the Trans-Catalina Trail. Initially, I was worried about the quality of the food I'd be eating on the trail since the complete overhaul on my nutrition post-diagnosis. I knew I needed to consume carbs (and sugar) to keep going on a long backpacking trip but I didn't fully understand what that meant as a newly diagnosed diabetic. My doctor assured me that I would be fine to eat what I normally pack on hikes and if anything, I should be more mindful of my sugar levels going too low since I'd be hiking all day, not too high.

Making our way up Cowles, I was worried about my blood sugar plummeting after hours of activity. I was worried I didn't pack the right snacks. I started to catch my thoughts wandering toward radically unlikely scenarios and stopped to take a breath and a sip of water. I had to remind myself of how far I've already come (before even setting foot on this trail) and give myself a little of the empathy that I so readily deliver for others.

"Sydney, you've lost nearly 60 pounds since you were diagnosed. You are in the best shape you've ever been in. The five-miler you did last week actually felt like a piece of cake, remember?"

As we approached the top, I told Barry "I don't think I'm going to be able to do this today if we don't eat between stops," continuing the conversation we had been having in my head (read: just me, freaking out about food by myself while silently marching up this mountain). He gently reminded me there was a deli across the street, and all of this park is surrounded by civilization, and we could probably find some food after we completed Cowles and Pyles.

I find that the first 15-30 minutes of any hike is my internal negotiations with myself. At some magical moment, my negative self-talk goes away and the bliss I find while hiking returns to me and I'll shout OH YEAH, I LOVE THIS. That's usually when Barry turns around and smiles and is like "YUP! We're just walking!" and all is well.

When we got to the summit, I was feeling much better and was excited to take pictures at the summit signs to signify my completion of this peak for the challenge.

#2: PYLES PEAK – RESPONSIBILITY

 Responsibility: People who are especially talented in the Responsibility theme take psychological ownership of what they say they will do. They are committed to stable values such as honesty and loyalty.

As we made our way over to Pyles Peak, the crowd thinned out again and I settled back into my head and got comfy exploring my thoughts again. I thought back to just a few minutes prior, where I was convinced that there wasn't food for me to eat around here and that surely, I'll die on this trail not even a few miles into it and giggled. My brain makes some pretty dramatic jumps sometimes.

When I took this strengths assessment, it was like a gigantic lightbulb going off at the responsibility section. Here's some more context on "psychological ownership":

This conscientiousness, this near obsession for doing things right, and your impeccable ethics, combine to create your reputation: utterly dependable. When assigning new responsibilities, people will look to you first because they know it will get done.

Say, for example, that you ask me to remind you to get carrots at the store. I say "okay! You got it!" and file that away. Then we go to the store, we go past the carrots, I'll probably even pick them up, but you walk right past them. There is a good chance that holding the carrots in my hand isn't enough to trigger the reminder, so I'll put them back down and keep shopping. Then we get back from the store and you're like "OH, I FORGOT THE DAMN CARROTS." At that moment, I physically recoil, and my stomach does a backflip. Not only did I tell you that I'd remind you about the carrots, but I held them IN MY HAND and let you down. I will start to figure out the master plan to make this up to you. This was how I processed every single situation ever in my life leading up to this realization. Sometimes it's great, sometimes it's problematic.

I smiled to myself, remembering that I'd be okay throughout this hike and I could trust that I know how to take care of myself. When I posted about this challenge on my Facebook page, I mentioned that Barry thought we could tackle this challenge in one day, and I remembered the comments where my ability to complete this hike was questioned. My pace quickened a bit, as did my breath. I felt a surge of energy of sorts, that part of my body that physically reacts to the accountability piece – and this time it was different.

Now, I'd be lying if I said there still wasn't a little piece of me that wanted to prove myself to the folks who assumed I couldn't do this. But that surge of energy I caught in this instance was all for me. I wanted to prove to *myself* that I could. Hold *myself* to my word. If I can get that upset about remembering carrots, I can surely direct some of that energy toward caring about my well-being.

I cheered myself on: *You said you wanted to do this in one day. You already bagged one peak, halfway up the second, and it's not even 9 a.m. You got this. Keep walkin'. Go get those summit selfies.*

And so it was.

#3: KWAAY PAAY - LEARNER

 Learner: People who are especially talented in the Learner theme have a great desire to learn and want to continuously improve. In particular, the process of learning, rather than the outcome, excites them.

This hike was the shortest distance to the summit of the five peaks we were tackling, 2.4 miles. The elevation gain was also the lowest of the segments we were tackling. So, when we got there and it was straight up, no switchbacks, with all the gain at once with no relief from the steep incline, I was taken aback. I started to feel my hip get a little tweaked like it did on that last summit before Blackjack campground on the Trans-Catalina Trail. I was wishing I had my trekking poles from the car so I could take a little pressure off. About halfway up, I turned around, took a few deep breaths and out of nowhere, a few tears started to well up. I was struggling with my Learner's tendency toward process: *In particular, the process of learning, rather than the outcome, excites them.* That part didn't sit well with me and triggered memories of being told "when shit gets hard, you run" on my way out of the startup. I had been trying to prove to myself that I don't run, and that part about the *process* being the part I liked (rather than the outcome) seemed to confirm the position.

Here's where my mind wandered: "When shit gets hard, you run."

Can I prove that true or false? If you look at my resume, what do you see? Chaos? Organized exploration?

- Marketing Coordinator/Bartender at a swanky steakhouse
- Student Brand Manager at Chipotle

- Intern at Moffitt Cancer Center
- Account Executive at a PR agency in Chicago
- Data Analyst at a marketing agency in Austin
- Competitive Skydiver / Director of Marketing in the skydiving industry at two different skydiving centers
- Ran my own skydiving events & marketing business
- Returned to the agency as Account Director, West/Central Leadership Team, working with global brands
- Co-Founder/CMO of an all-natural beauty brand

When we filmed my Diabetes documentary, the screening interviews helped me understand my story better. I had been on a journey for the past seven or eight years to figure out who I am, and what I'm supposed to be doing on this planet. Professionally, most of the bullet points have marketing as the common thread, as that was the function I was serving in each of those industries. But more than that, this is a demonstration of my love of learning. Marketing is something I'm good at, a skill I possess. I worked on building that skill and explored how that skill can be used in a variety of industries.

I've been told that my resume is both problematic and inspirational, so you can imagine how that might lead a girl to question what she's been doing for the last few years.

The takeaway from the Learner theme is that it's 100% okay for me to do things my way. My way has historically been "find an activity, get really saturated in it, learn as much as I can and/or acquire a particular level of understanding and then move on to the next thing."

I truly believe that life is a series of experiences strung together to teach you how to get the most out of the human experience. If you're paying attention, damn near every experience can teach you something about yourself or the world around you.

As I stood facing back toward where we parked, looking out over the park and the highways in the distance, I just absorbed all of it and let it seep into my bones.

#4: NORTH FORTUNA – INTELLECTION

 Intellection: People who are especially talented in the Intellection theme are characterized by their intellectual activity. They are introspective and appreciate intellectual discussions.

As we made our way through the grasslands to the Fortuna Saddle Trail, Barry and I were talking about how much our lives had changed since my diagnosis.

Barry said to me, "I could very well run this section, I feel like I could do that."

My response: "Me too!"

A few minutes later I chuckled to myself. Barry asked what was so funny.

"I never in my life thought we'd contemplate running together. That's all!"

Once we got to the Saddle Trail, it is one very steep fire road that takes you up to the peaks. No shade. Just a wide road with varying amounts of gravel on it, at points so steep it felt like an ice pick would have been helpful to navigate the dramatic incline.

There's a section of the Clifton Strengths assessment description of the "Intellection" theme that really stuck with me:

Chances are good that you prepare for important conversations or discussions by collecting lots of background information. It is not unusual for you to set aside at least five hours of quiet time each week to consider what you have discovered.

As we were approaching the summit, I felt a little nudge toward understanding: *"When you're all talked out, go hiking."*

Over the past few months, I had been leaning heavily on my friends and family for support through these transitions – from being an undiagnosed diabetic at my heaviest to the lightest I've ever been as an adult, from corporate life to startup life to this "follow your heart, make some art" chapter. I had been talking through a lot of things. I was spending countless hours on the phone working through my feelings, and by the time it was all over I made the decision to make room for adventure so I could find out what my purpose is. I was all talked out.

But I know myself, and I know that just because I'm all talked out doesn't mean I'm totally healed. The hike up to North Fortuna further connected the dots between coping mechanisms and diabetes and brought Hiking My Feelings into focus.

#5: SOUTH FORTUNA – ADAPTABILITY

 Adaptability: People who are especially talented in the Adaptability theme prefer to "go with the flow." They tend to be "now" people who take things as they come and discover the future one day at a time.

The only constant in life is change. I'm a walking example of embracing that, *and* it's incredible to look back and see how I've been resisting it. What I thought was one of my weaknesses has actually always been a strength, I just missed the signs.

For most of my adult life, I've worked in a high-stress career. Public relations is a stressful industry. Marketing is stressful. And doing that in an agency environment or the skydiving industry is stress on top of an already stressful career choice. Deciding to jump headfirst into the beauty industry in an attempt to change the conversation from the inside, while also jumping into entrepreneurship, while also jumping into raising venture capital – I clearly am not afraid of risks.

So why is it then, at almost every turn in my career, I inevitably feel like this just isn't a good fit? Is it that I've really internalized this American programming of DO MORE BE MORE HAVE MORE? Is it because I'm incapable of being satisfied? Am I wishy-washy?

Or, is it possible that I've been trying to fit a mold I wasn't designed to fit? Just because I'm really good at marketing doesn't mean that I need to be doing that exclusively, let alone for the rest of my life. Giving myself permission to sit with that reality has been a process of extending myself the same empathy I extend to others.

I mean, this was certainly the case for my health. I tried everything under the sun to lose weight before my diagnosis and I could never keep it off. Every time I set out to lose weight, I would ask my skinny friends what they were currently doing. Some of them were on a fad diet, some were combining diet pills, some worked out three hours a day, some just had good luck and good genetics.

What would follow was the same cycle, every time:

- Try something new.
- Do it obsessively until I see results.
- See results, be excited by results, reward myself with unhealthy food.
- Never return to activity that led to the results.
- Gain all the weight back and then some.

If it was possible for me to get diagnosed with Diabetes, go to the classes, review all the things I've done to get healthy in the past and throw it all away and follow my intuition to lose nearly 60 pounds, then perhaps it was possible that I had been making career choices from a place that was not aligned with what I actually want.

Perhaps, if I took the same refined approach to my career as I did to my health, I could finally find what I've been seeking, professionally.

That was heavy. And, like the whole "chasing dreams" thing, once I saw it, I couldn't unsee it.

At the summit of the first training hike, I realized that instead of eating and drinking my feelings in times of stress, I had been hiking my feelings. Diabetes was to thank for that. I felt empowered and having awareness around this shift was revolutionary for me.

However, while Hiking My Feelings felt like an interesting container for processing emotions, I have never been one to be satisfied with just one answer, so I wanted to get to the root of this. Why was I eating or drinking my feelings in the first place?

I had been doing a lot of journaling around this hiking my feelings idea and started posting my essays on my website, as well as some pictures on Instagram. Suddenly, my branding instincts kicked in - has anyone used this hashtag? Is the URL available? How about the Instagram handles? The hashtag hadn't been used before and the handle was available. So was the URL. I was shocked that someone else hadn't thought of this yet. I mean of course I wasn't the first person to find clarity on the trail, but it blew my mind that #hikingmyfeelings wasn't already a thing out there in the Universe.

It felt like a calling.

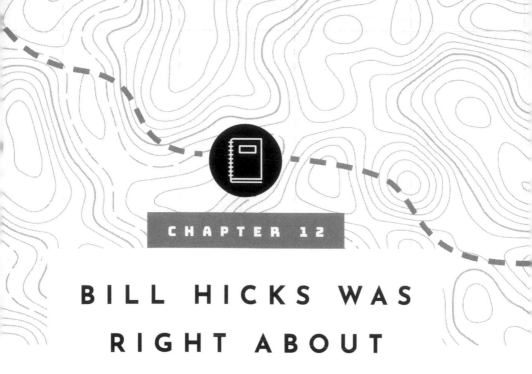

CHAPTER 12

BILL HICKS WAS RIGHT ABOUT EVERYTHING

The two weeks after I left the startup was a weird limbo space. I had been holding onto my work-issued laptop computer as collateral, which was hilarious considering I was owed close to $13,000 and the computer was worth $750.

Barry and I had been training for the Trans-Catalina Trail and we felt super prepared. I picked up some extra items to keep on me in case my blood sugar went low and ended up picking up a different pair of shoes for the trip so I could have a bit more grip.

On the day we were scheduled to leave San Diego to embark on our second journey across the island, we had an easy travel day planned. We got everything packed up the night before. Barry couldn't get out of his opening shift so it would be an early start for him. We planned on heading up to Long Beach in the afternoon, crashing with our friends again, then we'd wake up, take the 6 a.m. ferry to Avalon, and hit the trail.

We woke up early on June 1st, and I dropped Barry off at work. I drove back home, packed up the car with all of our gear, made some tea, lit some incense in my office, sat down in my big yellow chair, turned on my salt lamp, grabbed my journal, and started free-writing about the adventure that would start tomorrow.

FRIDAY, JUNE 1, 2018

"Tomorrow, our adventure on the Trans-Catalina Trail begins.

In this moment, I'm nervous AF. I weighed my bag and I'm comin' in hot at 30 pounds without water or the gimbal. I'm trying to cut weight but there's nothing left to cut, except food. Everything else is packed.

I also got paid today – the final balance Molly owes me. I am returning the computer before I pick up Barry. Pretty excited about that and glad all of this will be over by the time we leave.

THANK GOD.

Now that that cord will be cut, I'm interested to see how I feel once it is. This is going to be a doozy!

This trip is very symbolic in some regards. A break in my career. A break in the weight loss. I don't want to put too much pressure on this hike, so I'll say this:

I am excited to see what comes up for me, how it feels, where it comes from, and most importantly:

IS IT MINE?

I've realized that so much of what I experience day to day isn't mine. People projecting and reacting. Cosmic shit. Past life shit.

If nothing else, I want to take my time, enjoy the ride, and appreciate every step I am able to take.

If nothing else, I want to take a good look at whatever comes up and let myself explore whether it's mine or not, and then process accordingly.

If nothing else, I'm thrilled to have this time with Barry. We have been through a lot and it feels like an upswing and I am so grateful for his support.

If nothing else, I'm prepared to be in awe of my body. I have done some deep work to get to this point and the work continues on and off the trail. Truthfully, the majority of the "work" is mental, not physical. Just like this hike. Intensely physical, yes, but we're walking...

I closed my journal. Something nudged me to open it again. *Nope, not done.*

I continued,

I'm so thankful that I have Barry to share this with. Yesterday he was so kind to me, so gentle, while I was lying there crying. This whole thing feels like a lot.

Sometimes I find myself worried that I'm going to die before I'm ready. And sometimes, it doesn't sound too bad (to die). I want to keep track of this. I feel, intuitively, that most of those feelings will go away when I get on the trail, but if they don't, I want to note that. For a couple of reasons:

I can't bypass the talking part of my process and skip straight to hiking my feelings. Fortunately, I can walk and talk so that's why I'm so calm about it, but I want to be sure I acknowledge that I don't make a habit of putting off dealing with it until I'm on the trail. Otherwise, the trail could become a block, and I wouldn't want that.

I can prevent hating hiking, knowing the way I grew to hate skydiving, by honoring and enjoying my newness.

In skydiving, I always had one eye toward the podium. I didn't stay as present in the process as I could have, I always wanted to be better and was disappointed with what was.

With this, I am leaning heavily on my newbie status AND ALSO going to be paying attention to my limits and how I can push them, appropriately.

I closed my journal again. The urge to continue writing came back. I reopened my journal and continued;

Yesterday, I had the call with Jens and Alex [production team for the diabetes documentary we did in January 2018] and we are moving forward with the pilot of this new storytelling platform. I recorded my first video journal entry today and sent the link to Alex for review. We will see what they say!

I plan to do a video journal every morning, actually. I like the idea of that better than the idea of writing heavily. I'll keep a journal, of course, but primarily want to be fresh for video entries.

I'm pumped to run around Little Harbor on the 4th and just enjoy this body. I'm even going to ask Barry if he'll take pictures of me in my bikini when we get there. I don't want to have one single regret from this trip. NOT ONE! And that means asking for what I want, taking my time to take pictures, and savoring every moment.

This is the first week of my new life. Once I drop this computer off, I am FREE. I've always been free to be me, and this is hella exciting because now I know that. I don't need permission to already feel this way, but it's certainly going to feel official once we get through that. I don't have anything left to say to her. I think my parting words will be:

I'm excited to see you take this as far as I've always known you could.

Best of luck.

DEUCES!

Now it's time to hike my feelings, be confidently weird, and move toward my core desired feelings: Generous. Grounded. Joy.

I love me. I love Barry. I love fam. I love Kat. I love puggles.

See you on the other side.

I closed my journal again and I started thinking about how Adam wrote his mom a note about what to do if he dies before he went on the trip he never came home from. At the time, she thought that was so weird that he'd do that, but that letter ended up being the wishes we carried out at his memorial.

I opened the journal again. *Jesus, okay, let's wrap it up.*

...I had this weird wave come over me, and it felt like "see you on the other side" was super morbid.

To BE CLEAR!! I love this life and I'm excited to see where it goes

AND

It's okay that I'm scared of what comes next. The not knowing (more like not believing) is something I hope to work through on the trail because that shit is getting old. But now that I'm rabbit-holing here – if something happens to me or Barry on this trip and you found this journal, please tell our love story.

Talk about how Barry thought I was giving him googly eyes and for eight years I denied it. IT WAS TRUE. I DID. I loved him the moment I saw him.

Talk about how all we ever wanted, collectively and separately, was to be happy & free, because, for us, that's this hike. It's more hikes after this. It's writing books from our cabin in the woods, and hosting hikers who are thru-hiking the nearby trail. Trail angels. I want to be trail angels and I want to serve Kat's mac & cheese (the one Adam loved) and mochi to hikers. Plus, Barry's burgers. Shepherd's Pie. That freaking waffle, olive oil, sea salt combo for dessert.

I want to triple crown long distance hikes. With Barry.

I want us to figure out a way to turn our love story into a framework for the growth of humans – how to love ourselves and each other. Barry is such a good teacher and his visions for education in America are BEAUTIFUL.

I don't know why I feel like this has to get out, but I guess I'll just go with it.

FUCKING MORBID.

So yeah, trail angels who hike and raise goats and grow food and write books and take pictures and just have a place or community who can receive all this love we have to give.

I closed the journal again. *Nope, not done. GOOD GOD, WHEN WILL THIS END? WHAT IS HAPPENING?*

I continued;

I'm so excited to go to Norway with Dad, it's like a redemption tour of sorts. Our last trip together was rough. I've grown up a lot, and so has dad, tbh. I'm just really excited to see what is possible here. I'd love to help him turn his content into e-books and generate enough passive income for them so that they could do whatever they want. They deserve it.

I'm looking forward to adventures with Whitney and Bruno and spoiling their babies. I love that Whit and I are getting closer, and I love that she's been sharing stuff with me. Feels really nice.

I'm so excited for Kat – I feel like sometimes I'm a stage 5 clinger because she's so cool, and then I'm like "oh shoot, she's my sister from another mister" We've been friends for lifetimes. She's going to do amazing things because she's an incredible woman. I hope she sees and believes that soon.

And as far as Barry goes, the main reason I'm excited about this hike is I can finally, truly, 100% feel like I can see myself the way he's always seen me. I've said that before, but I didn't really get it until very recently. He is my rock and best friend and he gets me and somehow, he still loves me. I'm the luckiest woman in the world to have him to spend my life with. DAMNIT.

IDK why I'm crying but I hope we come home safe and this is all just a gratitude exercise and not a morbid letter.

Closed the journal again. Wiped the tears from my eyes.

I turned to a new page. "If I die," I started the new entry.

"*Cremate me and take me around the world. Barry knows the places,*" I wrote, tears streaming down my face.

I listed the places I wanted my ashes spread, a combination of places that are significant for me and Barry - where the creek that runs through

Limekiln State Park runs out to the ocean, Catalina Island, Sunset Cliffs - and places that we had talked about visiting but hadn't seen yet - Banff, Costa Rica, all the National Parks.

I continued;

> Maybe I'm saying bye to an old identity.
> Maybe I'm psychic AF and some bad shit is gonna happen.
> Maybe I'm psychic AF and I know that once I close this journal and put it down and load up the car and lock the door, I am forever changed.
> Maybe I am realizing the weight (and ease) of that.
> Maybe I finally know I'm going to be okay.
> Barry (and Bill Hicks) were right about everything.
> EVERYTHING.
> Hearts, sparkles, rainbows & unicorns,
> Sydney
> 2:04 p.m. PST
> 6/1/18
> 2 days until 33!

I closed the journal, put the cap on my pen, and picked up my phone. It was time to pick up Barry and hit the road.

The dogs would be staying home this time, so I made sure they had water and let them out one last time before I left, wrote a note for the dog sitter, and got in the car. I didn't have time to go to Molly's first, I needed to go get Barry. I picked him up, asked about his day, and went through all of the possible things I could say to Molly as I gave her the computer back. We pulled up to her place, and I walked up to the patio which was right by the gate to get into the building, just like I did every day I came to work. I felt myself get a bit nostalgic. I had visions of buying the last undeveloped lot on Sunset Cliffs boulevard, building a casita in the back for my parents, swimming in my money like Scrooge McDuck. The visions I had for this chapter of my life that would never come to fruition. She came out to greet me. Awkward small talk was exchanged, and I mentioned that we were headed to Catalina Island to hike the TCT again.

I handed her the computer and said, "have a lovely, lovely time."

I walked back to my car. *Smooooooth, Sydney. What does that even mean? My last words to one of my best friends are "have a lovely, lovely time?" Seriously?* I had played this exchange out so many times in my head and was ready for an epic monologue if the situation called for it. It was so anticlimactic. An unemotional end to an emotionally turbulent chapter of my life. A MacBook Air doesn't weigh much, as the name would indicate. But the second I handed off that computer, I felt lighter. I had a bit more pep in my step. Energetically, the cord was cut. That was the last connection I had to this woman and this business, and I was about to embark on the adventure of a lifetime, with nothing in my way while I was there, and nothing to return to when I got done hiking across the island. This was a clean slate, a fresh start, and I was going to take advantage of this opportunity.

I got back in the car, recounted the conversation to Barry, and just laughed.

"When a movie gets made about our lives, that scene will be so awkward," I thought to myself.

As we pulled onto the freeway, Barry looked at me and smiled; "You ready to have a great time?"

Yes, yes I was.

"Catalina, here we come!" I said, looking out the window at nothing in particular, lost in my own thoughts.

It was time to start a new adventure.

CHAPTER 13

HOT SAGE

The drive up to Long Beach was uneventful and traffic wasn't nearly as bad as it was the last time we drove to Catalina. We stayed with the same friends as we did before the first trip. This time, they had twin babies on the way. We hopped in the car and went to a restaurant near their old house, the one we used to party at back when we were all skydiving. We took turns filling in the gaps between what we post on social media and what else happened in our lives over the past few months, had a quick dinner, and returned to the house to crash before our early start.

We filled up our water bladders for the next day, set out our hiking clothes, scheduled a Lyft to pick us up, set our alarms, and went to bed.

I woke up to my phone vibrating. It was the Lyft driver, he was outside. *Shit shit shit shit shit, we missed our alarm!*

I told the Lyft driver we'd be right down and asked him to wait for us.

I woke Barry up and it was a mad dash to get into our hiking clothes, gather our belongings, and make our way downstairs. By the time we got there, the driver had already left. I opened the app to catch another ride.

Our ferry was at 6 a.m., this was not the way I wanted to start the trip.

The minutes that passed between requesting the ride and when our driver actually showed up were some of the longest minutes of my life. When the driver got there, we put our backpacks in the back, sat down and buckled up.

"I see you're headed to the ferry, what's up with the backpacks?" he asked.

"Yes, we're supposed to catch the 6 a.m. ferry so we can hike across the island this week. We missed our first ride so if you can get us there in time, I'll seriously love you forever, man!"

"You got it!" he said as the car accelerated.

A few minutes passed before he spoke up again.

"So, hiking across the island, huh? That sounds awesome. If I wanted to do something like that, I'd have to go with one of my buddies. How cool that you guys get to do this together, you're so lucky."

I put my hand on Barry's knee and shot him a look.

"Baaaaabe, we're so lucky," I cooed.

Barry smiled and rolled his eyes.

We made it to the ferry in time to go to the restroom and get in line to board the ferry. We scanned the line and didn't see very many backpackers. As if on cue, the guy behind us asked us if we were hiking the TCT.

"Yes indeed, it's our second time!" I was a walking exclamation point with my early bird enthusiasm. Everything was exciting. We made it to the ferry on time, I'm waiting in line, it's not going anywhere without me, life is good, and this trip has officially begun.

"When was your first trip?" he asked.

"December 2016, between Christmas and New Year's."

"Ah yes, the rain event!" he said, referring to the downpour we experienced that second night in Little Harbor.

Barry and I both laughed.

"Yeah, that was brutal," Barry said.

The guy behind us continued, "Well, they've made some changes to the trail since then, more shade structures, more restrooms, and some rerouting at different points along the trail."

He introduced himself as an employee of the Catalina Island Company, the parent company for mostly everything on the island as far as hospitality is concerned. We chatted for a few more minutes, and a big group of backpackers got in line behind us. Our new friend let us know that they hosted a Trans-Catalina Trail trip and he said it was super luxurious as far as backpacking goes. They did the trail in three days versus our six-night itinerary, but they set up your camp for you, cook your meals for you, and haul your gear. All you have to do is walk and carry a daypack with snacks and water.

Well that sounds like the perfect environment for hiking my feelings. I thought to myself.

The line started to move; it was time to go.

"Enjoy your hike!" he said as we started to board the ferry.

Once on board, Barry and I dropped off our bags and made our way to the back deck. The sun was starting to rise, and we wanted to get some good pictures on the way into the harbor at Avalon.

As we motored out of the harbor, I was flooded with memories of our first trip, and when we first moved to Southern California. Once we started picking up speed toward the island, I saw a cruise ship in the distance and smiled. I snapped a few photos for my dad and vowed to remember to send them to him after the trip.

We got to the island and the buzz was the same. We grabbed our bags, started making our way through town, and tried not to get lost this time.

We passed the mile 1 marker by the golf course when we heard someone shouting. There was a golfer on the green asking us what we're doing with the backpacks. We informed him that we are hiking across the island and he was floored.

"Wait what? You can hike across the whole island? You've inspired me, I'm going to do that!" he shouted at us from the other side of the fence.

I looked at Barry and laughed.

"Baaaaabe, we're lucky, we're inspiring, what else is possible here?"

We made our way past the golf course to Hermit Gulch, the campground at the start of the trail. We double checked water, put on sunscreen, moved snacks around to be easily accessible, and went to the bathroom. I grabbed a Planet Green Socks sticker and put it on the trashcan.

Adam is with us on this trip, too. I thought to myself.

I checked my blood sugar, and it was a bit higher than I'd like for it to be at that hour, but with all the stress that morning, to be expected. After I put my glucometer back in my bag, we geared up again and started making our way out of Hermit Gulch.

"We should totally come a day early next time we do this trail; camp here, and then wake up and roll out," I said.

Starting the morning in a flurry of stress and missed rides was not my ideal way to kick off this trip, but I had already shaken that off. Point was, it's an early start no matter how you slice it, and this first day on-trail in the hardest, I already knew that much. It was a gorgeous day, mid-60's at the start of the hike, with temperatures forecasted to be in the mid-70's to low 80's all week. Not a drop of rain in sight.

I paused to take a sip of water and look around. *This spot looks really familiar.* I closed my eyes and open them again. *Yep, this is the place where I had to tape up my hotspot on the first trip.* Now that I had a bit more experience with this hiking thing, I pulled out my tracking app. I thought for sure it was at least an hour and a half or two hours before I had to pull over last time.

DISTANCE: 0.25 MILES

I called ahead to Barry.

"BABE! This is where I had to pull over last time! Guess how far we are!"

Silence.

"We're a quarter mile in!"

I heard laughter and could see him shaking his head.

I had asked myself before we started this journey, *"what would be possible if the hike itself wasn't the hard part?"*

I was starting to think maybe I was psychic after all.

We kept trucking up the switchbacks and made it to the first shade structure.

I looked at Barry as he took his pack off.

He's lost weight. He looks incredible. He's like a billy-goat up these switchbacks and I'm keeping up just fine. This is a different hike, that's for sure.

We sucked down water, I reapplied sunscreen, and I busted out my DSLR. I didn't want my camera to become the Tarot Cards of the first trip, so I took it out and snapped pictures every chance I could.

We packed it up and kept going. The stretch after the first shade structure was mostly flat, but I knew what was coming. On the flat parts of the trail, the hiking was quiet and mindless, just the way I like it. It was a beautiful day for hiking, the sun was shining, birds were singing, a nice light breeze blowing when we came around the bend to face the ocean, life was good. As we passed the place where I took that first full body shot on the first trip, I started crying. We made our way through the gate that warns you about bison territory and descended into a canyon with fields of sage as far as the eye could see. I remembered this section from the first hike, and as we made our way further into the canyon, as the day wore on, the plants started to heat up. Every once in a while, I'd catch a breeze and with it, a whiff of sage.

"BABE! IT SMELLS LIKE SAGE! LIKE HOT SAGE!" I shouted ahead to Barry.

After a nice cruise through some of the canyon floor, we started to climb out of that canyon and into the next. As we did, Barry shouted back to me, "Shifting down a gear!"

He says this every time the trail gets steeper and it's one of my favorite things and also drives me crazy. It's my favorite because he does it and it's adorable and I always pretend I'm driving a stick shift and motion my hand as if I'm shifting down. It drives me crazy because he's usually a good bit ahead of me, and I could be in the middle of feeling really awesome, but the second the idea of a steeper climb enters my awareness, my whole body slumps a bit. In this case, when he called back, I was already stopped. I had my hands on my knees, silently screaming as tears were pouring down my face. Here's the rabbit hole I went down after smelling the sage:

The whiff of sage I caught smelled delicious, and potent. My brain made the jump to my uncle Mike, who died in 2014. He used to split this time between New York and San Francisco, and for the holidays, sometimes he'd come back to Kansas and surprise everyone. On one particular Christmas, Mike was staying with us at our house. He took over my sister's room and when he left, her room reeked of clove cigarettes. I thought it was so rude that he'd smoke in the house, but Dad later told us that he was smoking weed and that the cloves masked the smell. I followed that memory as far as it would go - all of Mike's business ventures, his creativity, his spirit, his singing voice.

I hadn't really had a chance to properly grieve his death. He was a ward of the state and died in a hospice house. There was no funeral. My aunt got his remains and sent some of them to my dad in an aluminum, resealable Coca-Cola bottle. That was it. This beautiful bright light was reduced to ashes in a soda bottle.

I thought of all the times Mike's creativity was spoken of in a negative way. For most of my adult life, my father had referred to my uncle as this beacon of hope for the gay community, while also reminding us to go to college, get degrees, and get real jobs. That a life of creativity and performing wasn't going to make us happy because we wouldn't have money. It's almost like we were supposed to embody Mike's spirit but cut our creativity off at the knees.

I looked up to Barry, still keeled over with my hands on my knees.

I waved, signaling I was okay. By now Barry was well aware of what can happen with me on the trail. He's seen this before. I reassured him I was fine and told him not to wait for me, that I needed a minute. He kept going and I stayed where I was. I let it all out. I had an experience like this on the first trek across the island - this felt more like an exorcism than anything I had control over. Screaming silently, with nothing coming out, like when I was in the shower during a panic attack. Like when we found out Chris died and I crumpled up on the kitchen floor, and then when we were driving to the drop zone after found out he killed himself. It felt like when I finally heard back about Adam and got confirmation that he was dead. Standing keeled over on this trail, it felt like I was having an out of body experience, remembering where I was when I found out all of these friends died. LA Fitness for Jonathan. In the kitchen for Chris. Driving when we get the text about Stephanie. Reeling from Graham's death when we found out Tom died. On the DZ when they found Marius. On the DZ when Ken died. At dinner when Larry died. Sitting on the steps when we heard about Avishai. Blow after blow after blow.

*Taking a break to stretch and reflect on this
bench at Haypress Reservoir.*

At the beginning of this book, I shared that I lost a few folks in 2014, but in the four years I was a skydiver, 23 of my friends died. In this moment on the trail, I moved the grief all the way out of my body for every single one of them.

When I resumed hiking, I thought about each person individually. What was my favorite memory with them? What did they mean to me? How could I keep their legacy alive? I spent most of my time looking at the ground, picking my head up every so often to see what was coming and making sure I could still see Barry. For miles, I hiked and processed and remembered and cried and threw up and dry heaved and laughed and keeled over, like I had earlier, silently screaming with my head between my knees, as if braced for impact.

When I looked up again, I saw the playground coming into view. Our halfway point.

I picked up the pace to catch up to Barry, feeling lighter in my shoes. When we got to the playground, I slung my pack off my shoulders and grabbed my glucometer from the top pocket. My blood sugar was a little elevated earlier, and I attributed it to the stress of missing my alarm and the first Lyft. I had been concerned about my nutrition and hydration for this trip, and this was the first time I checked my blood since we got on the trail.

I unzipped my glucometer, picked a test strip out of the container, and inserted it into the top of the device. While it turned on, I took the finger pricking component, put my thumb on the button that "cocks" the lancet, drew it back until it clicked, and pricked my finger. The blood had no trouble coming through the skin, I was bleeding like a stuck pig. I put a drop on the test strip and closed my eyes.

Please be good, please be good, please be good. It would be so nice to not have to worry about my blood sugar on this trip.

My reading came back. It was perfect. I breathed a sigh of relief and showed Barry.

"That's great, baby! Congratulations!"

I turned off the glucometer, put it back in its case and put the case back in my bag. I took off my shirt, grabbed my water bladder, and made my way over to the faucet to fill it up.

Last time we were here, it was just me and Barry. I got on the swings and did everything I could to delay so I could cool down and give my legs a rest. This time, I felt incredible. I skipped over to the water fountain and started filling up my bladder. Behind me was a group of people. As I filled up my water, it hit me.

I was standing at the faucet in my trail runners, trekking tights, a sports bra, and no shirt.

Sydney Williams doesn't run around with her shirt off. I may have been a cheerleader, gymnast, athlete, but my stomach is the part of my body that I was most self-conscious about, the part of my body that was *always* covered up. What was happening here? I felt like I must have blacked out after the good blood sugar reading, because here I was in all of my shirtless glory, feeling the breeze blow across the skin on my bare belly for possibly the first time in my entire life.

It was such a strange sensation, to feel my body cooling down naturally. As the breeze caressed my sweaty back, I felt chills run up and down my spine.

I made my way over to where we dropped our stuff, put my bladder back in my bag, and went to sit on a bench to consider what just happened.

As I sat down and stretched out, I tried to make sense of what was happening here.

Okay, so no blisters, that's good. Blood sugar is on point. Water is full. I cried A LOT back there. Sitting here, I feel lighter, I've got an extra pep in my step. I'm not wearing a shirt and I'm not running to hide my body or cover up. How is that possible?

I thought of all the things I've passed on, for fear of my body being seen; my high school reunion, fun trips to the beach, wearing clothes appropriate for the weather or season - shorts and tank tops, specifically.

What happened here? Yes, I lost weight, but I don't think that's it. Last time I was here, it was just me and Barry, there's no reason I shouldn't have taken off my shirt then, but I didn't.

I wasn't sure what was happening here, but I was eager to get to the campground so I could write some more and see if I could connect the dots. Barry didn't have to tap his wrist this time. As soon as I finished some of my electrolyte chews, I geared up and we hit the trail again.

I knew we had at least one more big climb, the one where I had to stop every four steps on our last hike on the island. I was looking forward to it, I wanted to see how different it felt. We hiked through more sage fields, took a break in the one shady spot on this portion of the trail to suck down more water, and before I knew it, we were looking up at the last tough climb.

Last time we did this section of the trail, we got lapped by people we had never seen on the hike before. This time, we knew we were ahead of the group we ran into at the playground, but we hadn't seen anyone else yet.

I looked at the hill, checked my shoelaces, and made sure my gear was comfortable. It was go-time.

I made my way up the last switchbacks, remembering how last time I was dragging my leg and literally chanting *"right foot, left foot"*.

I started out a bit aggressively, thinking I could maintain that pace. I was wrong. I slowed down and remembered my core desired feelings: Generous. Grounded. Joy.

Generous, I said, taking a step. In this next chapter of my life, I wanted to feel generous with my time and talent.

Grounded, I said, taking another step. I wanted to prioritize feeling grounded. What helps me achieve that sense of calm that I so desire in my life?

Joy, I said, taking another step. I wanted to prioritize joy. I wanted to say yes more. I wanted to bring joy to others.

This time, I could take about 10-12 steps before I needed to pause and catch my breath, a marked improvement over the 3-4 steps I could take before I felt like I was going to vomit.

I kept my mantra going, even after the hard part was over.

Generous. Grounded. Joy.

Generous. Grounded. Joy.

I could see the campground. I was so hot, I was ready to take this shirt off again, put my head under the faucet at the campsite, and cool all the way down.

When I saw our campsite, I started skipping.

I could go to the bathroom! I could eat! I'm so excited to sleep! I wonder what time it is!

We slung our packs off our shoulders onto the bench of the picnic table. I grabbed my Nalgene and chugged it. When I finished, I took my phone out of my pocket and paused my tracking app.

"Babe, we got here two hours faster than we did last time!" I called over to Barry as he was unpacking his food options.

"Oh, hell yes!" Barry exclaimed, running over to me for a high five.

I busted out my miniature journal and grabbed my phone. I wanted to jot down the details of today before I forgot.

I had brought a very small and thin Moleskine notebook to keep notes in this time versus the big clunky journal I brought last time. On the previous trip I was trying to do big long journal entries and it started to feel like more of a burden in the moment, so I stopped. I wish I had kept better notes of that first trip, so for this trip I switched it up. At the bare minimum, I wanted to take notes on what I experienced, so I answered the same questions every day. If I felt like writing more, awesome, if not, totally fine, but I'd take note of the following things:

1 Statistics for the day - distance, time on trail, blood sugar readings, calories burned
2 What were my biggest wins?
3 What lesson(s) did I learn?
4 What am I thankful for right now?
5 How am I feeling right now?
6 What did I see/hear?
7 Did anything stand out?
8 Did I use any specific mantras today?

TCT JOURNAL ENTRY

June 2, 2018
Steps: 28,741
Miles: 11.16 on MapMyRun
Time: 7 hours
Calories burned: 4,329
Bison: saw 2 en route to Blackjack
@Blackjack!

We arrived almost two hours earlier than last time, holy shit. The last two summits before BJC were INSANE still, but I'm in way better condition upon arrival than I was last time. Bringing my DSLR was a good choice. Tomorrow is my 33rd birthday, holy poop! Today I repeated my core desired feelings with my steps: Generous. Grounded. Joy. So far, so good! Having chicken & dumplings for dinner, yay! Let's eat!

BIGGEST WINS:

✓ Shaved two hours off our time, feel freaking great, mostly happy tears today.

LESSONS LEARNED:

✓ My stories are mine to tell. Tell them, stop comparing or worrying.

THANKFUL FOR:

✓ That this is something Barry and I can share. We are so lucky.

HOW AM I FEELING:

✓ Grounded.

✓ Toes are sore, but not nearly the shit show we had last time.
✓ Back is a bit sore.
✓ Mentally, incredible. I love being out here.

WHAT DID I SEE/HEAR:

✓ At one point I accessed pure joy and bliss. All the sounds disappeared, and I was warm and free and sobbing. Did I die?

WHAT STOOD OUT:

✓ How much easier this is this time

MANTRAS:

✓ Generous. Grounded. Joy.
✓ I can do the hard things.
✓ Get it together, Williams!
✓ HOT SAGE!

I closed the journal and tucked it back into my backpack. Barry was done boiling water for his dinner, so now it was my turn. Chicken and dumplings. A Blackjack tradition for me at this point.

I scarfed down dinner and grabbed my camera to wander around the campground. We were in the campsite next to the one we were in last time, and I grimaced at the memory of what my feet were feeling like that first night on the trail in 2016. At that point, I had a blister on my heel, and my pinky toes had turned to blisters too. Barry was setting up the tarp so we could cowboy camp under the tree. I checked the angle of the portable solar panel I brought and was impressed by how it was charging the power brick to keep our cameras charged. Everything was going exactly how I imagined it would: I felt strong, I had a few really good cries and moved some energy out of my body, and this sunset was looking pretty magical.

The way the light was peeking through the trees up near the bathrooms caught my eye and I found myself skip-sprinting up the hill with my camera to try to get the shot before the light changed. Last time we were here, I couldn't even get up the hill to go to the bathroom. I made it up to the top of the hill and started taking pictures of a dead tree that was perfectly aligned with the Trans-Catalina Trail sign. I paused for a minute and just took a good slow look around. I wanted to remember every detail of this place, of this whole trip. I thought back to the pure bliss state that I found on the trail. I found that place after we left the playground, before we started that last climb. I noted the shift in my mindset.

After I cried so hard, I was keeled over, I felt lighter.

When I was filling up my water bladder, I felt confident.

And on that last climb before Blackjack, I felt inspired.

What was happening here? And what will tomorrow bring?

CHAPTER 14

BISON CHIPS

I had never cowboy camped before and I woke up for day two on the TCT super refreshed. It was my birthday and the plan was as follows; stop at the airport to grab something to eat, make our way down to Little Harbor, and celebrate my birthday that night and the whole next day on our day off.

As the sun rose and Barry started to make breakfast, I grabbed my camera and started wandering around the campsite.

"Sydney, turn around," Barry shout-whispered at me.

I didn't know what to expect, and I wasn't sure I heard him right. He motioned for me to turn around.

I turned around and there it was: a bison, no more than 75 feet away from us on the opposite side of the trail that leads up to the campground.

I had my camera in my hand, so I zoomed in as far as I could and took some pictures. I was so still and so quiet that the shutter on my camera sounded like thunder. I didn't want to spook him, so I slowly lowered my camera and tried to make picture memories in my mind. I watched as he grazed on the grasses and moved toward a patch of vegetation and trees near the restrooms. Once he was out of sight, I turned back to Barry and said: "Happy birthday to me!"

Birthday breakfast with bison at Blackjack, I thought, giggling to myself.

We finished our breakfast and packed up camp, heading toward Little Harbor. As we rounded the corner from the bathroom to get back on the trail, we saw the bison again. He was just off the side of the trail, maybe 30 feet from us. We moved off to our left, taking a wide route off the trail to give plenty of space between ourselves and the bison. Once the coast was clear, we got back on the trail and started laughing.

"Was that the same bison?" I asked Barry.

"Yup! Don't say I never got ya nothin' for your birthday!"

We made our way out of Blackjack campground and descended into the canyon that separates Blackjack from the Airport in the Sky. I remembered this part of the hike was brutal last time because my toes kept squishing into the front of my boots, making me wince with each step. This time felt like a normal hike, and as we passed the TCT sign on our way into the heavily wooded part, I posed by the sign with both hands showing three fingers for 33 years old. HAPPY BIRTHDAY TO ME!

We started climbing out of the canyon before the airport, passing the soapstone.

Good lord, I was so out of shape last time, how did we get as far as we did without dying or getting seriously injured? I thought to myself.

As we rolled into the airport, I felt my stomach grumble.

Oh no, not again. I was thinking about the literal shitstorm that happened last time I ate here.

As I looked at the menu, it was a hard pass on the buffalo burger, so I went with a BLTA. It was perfect. Last time I heard wild things about the cookies at the Airport in the Sky, so I picked one up to have for my

birthday dessert after dinner when we got to Little Harbor. We knew
Sheep Chute road was coming so we didn't waste any time. As we passed
the areas where I had to take an emergency poop the last time we did
this part of the trail, I was so damn thankful that I was feeling good. We
were cruising, making really good time, when we came up on the group
we had seen the day before. Were they at the airport when we were there?
Did they bypass it? Did they start earlier than we did? I didn't remember
seeing them at the campground in the morning and I definitely didn't see
them at the airport. We turned toward Sheep Chute Road and the guide
called out to us.

"Hey, if you're doing the TCT, the trail has changed!"

I stopped and turned around, walking back toward him. Barry pulled
out the map.

They were right. Sheep Chute Road wasn't part of the TCT anymore.
I felt a pang of panic. I didn't know what was ahead. I was prepared for
Sheep Chute, was this new section going to be harder?

"Pass us here, and around that corner you'll see a sign for Big Springs
Ridge Trail, can't miss it."

We thanked them and kept hiking. My panic heightened. What was this
section like? Why didn't I look at the map after that guy said the trail
changed? Shit.

I took a deep breath. *Everything is okay.* I was hot, gasping for air, and
feeling a bit panicky. I had packed a cooling towel and that sounded like
exactly what the doctor ordered. I took off my hat, draped the damp towel
over my head, and put my hat back on. As the breeze whipped around my
neck, it felt like personal air conditioning.

"Oh, wow that's so much better," I sighed.

"TOTAL GAME CHANGER," Barry shouted, his towel in a similar
configuration.

We found Big Springs Ridge Trail and I asked Barry to take a picture of me by the sign. As I looked ahead to the trail, I could see where Little Harbor was hiding in the marine layer. The trail itself was a gorgeous single-track, cut into the side of this mountain with tall grass swaying in the breeze. I saw the grass swaying before I felt the breeze pass through the towel, cooling me down again.

"Oh shit, I could get used to this!" I cheered as we started hiking.

Everything was gorgeous. Actual single-track, not deeply rutted fire roads. A hiker-friendly descent into Little Harbor, not this super aggressive road that jacked Barry's knees so good last time that he had to take the trail walking backward. This was hiking luxury. I felt like Julie Andrews in the Sound of Music.

We continued through grassy mountainside, over some exposed rock, and crested the final hill before our descent into the campground. I could see Little Harbor, the whale's tale, and Shark Harbor. We passed through rock piles and cairns, and I watched the marine layer burn off before my very eyes.

We are making incredible time, I thought to myself.

The campground started to come into view, and we could see the campsite we were at last time during the rainstorm. I was a good distance behind Barry. I was overcome with gratitude for how much better this hike was feeling, and I was peaceful in my state of moving meditation. I heard Barry shout something, breaking my daze, so I picked up my pace to catch him. As I came up behind him, he started singing happy birthday. I started crying.

We wandered around the campground and realized we were on the lower campground, closer to the beach. I was so stoked. This was the best birthday ever; woke up, took some awesome photos, saw a bison for my birthday breakfast, saw the bison again on our way out of the campground, got a BLTA, didn't shit myself, what else was possible? This was a dream!

We found our campsite and assessed the sleeping situation. We didn't bring the tent but given how close we were to the ocean at this site, we knew we didn't want to wake up all moist from the sea breeze. Barry made a lean-to style tent, stringing the tarp up between trekking poles.

Ugh, I love seeing this man in his element, I thought. *So sexy!*

The hike into Little Harbor was a quick one compared to the first day on the trail, so we had plenty of daylight to kill. I set up the solar panel on the picnic table, plugged in the brick, and changed into my bikini. Time to get my pictures.

Walking down to the beach, I thought of all the times I had wanted to be at a beach in a bikini but didn't feel comfortable enough to enjoy it. I had spent so much time covered up after the assault, to buy that one piece and love myself in it was such a shift. Buying this bikini after was a totally different ball game. My favorite perfect one piece didn't fit anymore. Now it was too long for me, and the crotch of the suit hung below my actual crotch. I went in there knowing exactly what I wanted: something sporty that was both cute and practical for paddleboarding and being active in the water.

Looking through the rack, I grabbed a large and medium first. I put the large on and it was too big.

Wow, I have lost weight.

I slid into the mediums. My butt, as I knew it, had left the building. Where my juicy cheeks used to live, pancakes now resided.

I need to build a new butt, I chuckled to myself.

Not judging, no hatred, just observations about this new body. It felt like the first time I was in the dressing room. Once again, I didn't recognize this body. Once again, I was curious about how I got here. This time I knew I had been working hard, managing diabetes via a complete lifestyle change, and the weight had melted off pretty quickly.

I looked at myself, noting the parts of my body that were different. My arms were more toned, as was my back, thanks to paddleboarding. My legs were much thinner and starting to develop some definition, and, was that, wait…. No, it couldn't be. My thighs weren't rubbing together anymore. *Do I have a thigh gap?* My mind went into overdrive.

Where are the free drinks?

Do I get more signatures in my yearbook now?

Will Stephen pay attention to me now?

Are there men beating down the door to come ask me on a date?

Who are these fellas? Can't they see I'm off the market?

Versions of me at 12, 16, 18, 21, and 28 all had questions.

Here I was, thin enough by my own standards to feel confident enough to buy a bikini. For the first time in a long time, I didn't talk myself out of it. So younger me was cautious to celebrate. She wanted to make sure the universe delivered on the other promises that we were chasing every time we set out on a weight-loss mission.

Thin girls get more friends, and thus, more yearbook signatures.

Stephen appears to like the skinny girls in our class.

Thin girls get free drinks.

And lots of dates.

And a husband.

I broke the news to Younger Me and assured her that we were doing just fine in all of those departments, and the only thing that matters is that we are happy, healthy, and kind. And right now, in this season of our lives, we were checking all three boxes. Sometimes, we won't be checking all three. Sometimes, it will be hard to check any boxes at all. I told her we didn't need to measure in quantity, that quality was more important here.

Having a few good friends who really know you and love you is better than trying to be everything to everyone.

Some boys won't like you back, and it will hurt, but you'll be okay. You can always love yourself and pay attention to yourself.

There's more to life than free drinks, just trust me on this one.

The folks you want to be spending time with will love you, first and foremost, and they'll understand that your body is a vehicle for that bright and sparkly soul of yours. Your size will fluctuate and as long as you're happy and you feel good, ultimately nothing else matters.

Younger Me had a moment, looking Current Me up and down.

"Well done, sis. Way to take care of us."

As I got closer to the water, I considered turning around and asking Barry to join me, but I was feeling shy and didn't want to bother Barry while he set up the tent, so I found myself a spot with the rock formation and ocean in the background, shoved the GoPro into the sand and turned on the camera to take some pictures of myself.

Pretending to be super casual while taking GoPro selfies on the beach.

The first one I took was perfect.

Great, I thought to myself, *now I won't get caught being a total weirdo over here!*

TCT JOURNAL ENTRY

June 3, 2018
Blackjack to Little Harbor
Distance: 8.48 miles on MMR
Calories burned: 2488

BIGGEST WINS:

✓ Not getting mauled by bison
✓ change in trail for the better, new leg is gorgeous and much
  more hiker-friendly
✓ Barry singing happy birthday on our way into campground
✓ body feeling incredible
✓ Barry starting a fire from nothing, with no fire to start fire
  HOT HUSBAND ALERT

LESSONS LEARNED:

✓ cold towels save lives
✓ wildlife is neat
✓ more confidence around my story + weight loss
✓ some things aren't as hard as they seem

WHAT AM I THANKFUL FOR?

✓ a body that continues to amaze me with what is capable of
✓ Barry's question about if I had to do this by myself, would
  I? I think I could with more training, but I don't know if

I'd want to, because I really enjoy sharing this with him. Perhaps that is something worth investigating?

HOW AM I FEELING RIGHT NOW?

- ✓ Physically: not sore, but tired.
- ✓ Mentally: a mix of complete Zen clarity and also existential dread that just came out of nowhere.
- ✓ Spiritually: grounded AF

WHAT DID I SEE/HEAR:

- ✓ Buffalo at blackjack campground
- ✓ petting zoo deluxe at our campsite; deer, foxes, squirrels, birds, etc. It was crazy.

WHAT STOOD OUT:

We have come so far. The trail change was so gorgeous and we're more capable of handling ourselves, which comes from letting go of a lot of bullshit. Whether that's the weight we carry daily, or losing weight in our packs, metaphorically and literally, it feels good. I'm surprised I don't feel like there is more to leave out here.

Maybe I'm realizing that I was whole when I got here and I'll be whole when I leave, and I don't NEED this to be some big thing, because by the very nature of it happening, it is a big thing.

MANTRAS?

- ✓ Generous. Grounded. Joy. ITS MY BIRTHDAY!!

After my solo photoshoot and journal time, we made dinner and went on an expedition.

Our mission: acquire bison chips. Poop. Bison poop. We were looking for piles of bison poop. We read that they make a great fuel source for a fire, so we took a lap around the campground and picked up dried piles of bison poop. It sounds gross, but really, it's just digested grass, there isn't much else to it. When we got back to the campsite, there were some dried out palm fronds on the ground beneath the tree near our tent. I started to look around and collect anything that could possibly make for good fuel for the fire. Barry started working on the fire as I got the water boiling for our dessert: raspberry chocolate crumble. Sounds fancy, it's not really. It's a mix of dehydrated raspberry puree plus a packet of crushed up chocolate cookies to mimic an Oreo crust. We had this on our first trip, and I was stoked to have something sweet for my birthday. This was one of the first desserts I had since I was diagnosed with Diabetes, and I was excited for the occasion.

As the water started to come to a boil, Barry started shouting about the fire he started. I looked around and saw the lighter on the table. *Wait a minute. How did he do that?*

He had dug deep beyond the surface ash and found some embers from a fire the night before. I thought it was pure magic. The fire burned pretty hot through the smaller timber, and the logs we found behind the tree at our campsite lit pretty quickly. As the sunset faded and the stars came out, Barry started placing the buffalo chips around the embers. As they caught fire, they went straight to smoldering. It smelled like mezcal - ashy, but a bit floral and vegetal.

We sat by the fire, passing a bag of raspberry crumble back and forth between us. Barry turned on his headlamp to grab another palm frond and as he panned the area around our campsite, he saw a bunch of animal eyes. We saw squirrels scamper away. A deer and her baby. A couple Catalina Island foxes - a species of fox you can only find on

Catalina Island, nowhere else in the world. It was wild. We were only under the tarp, so we made sure we put everything that wasn't a pillow, sleeping pad or sleeping bag in the bear box. We didn't want any visitors in the tent.

The next morning was our day off, and I had big plans. The last time we had a day off here, I was stuck on a picnic table drawing tarot cards about the year ahead and lancing blisters. This time, I wanted to explore. It was overcast and this side of the island was a bit chilly, so we bundled up, took our time making breakfast, and walked over to our campsite from the first trip.

They very well could have changed the layout between 2016 and this trip, but once we got up there, I looked at the tree we slept under on the night of the rainstorm and over across the road to where the porta potties were. It didn't seem that far. I mean, I could barely walk on that trip and every step took the effort of 10 with my cinder-block feet, but I couldn't help but giggle to myself.

We joked about the bison prints looking like Jurassic Park, my Lady Gaga-style muddy hiking shoes and rain gear ensemble, and the poor trail conditions.

As we walked down to the whale's tale rock formation, I knew which photos I wanted. I wanted Outdoor Goddess Standing on a Rock Looking at the Ocean - and this was the place to do it. I looked at what I was wearing: trail runners, my green socks I got in memory of Adam, black trekking tights, a neon blue long sleeve, a purple vest, and a grey beanie. This is quite the look, especially for the first week of June on an island.

I didn't care - I rocked that little photo shoot. Mismatched clothes and all. We spent the rest of the day taking pictures at Shark Harbor, watching the waves, exploring more of the rock formations, and sitting on the beach near our campsite.

As the sun started to set, I pulled out my notebook and re-read my entry from my birthday.

Maybe I'm realizing that I was whole when I got here and I'll be whole when I leave, and I don't NEED this to be some big thing, because by the very nature of it happening, it is a big thing.

I sat there; in awe of the clarity I had found. *Hiking my feelings, indeed.* I grinned to myself. I read that part over and over, really trying to wrap my head around what wholeness felt like in this moment. So far, I had some pretty high highs and was moving a lot of old energy through my body. Something was clearly happening here. *Was this island magic? Did I die on the way here and is this heaven?*

We started another fire and talked about the remaining sections of the trail. We knew the climb out of Little Harbor to get back to the ridgeline was tough, and there were at least two if not three ridgelines before you get to start making the way down into Two Harbors. As for the rest of the trail out to Parsons Landing and back, we didn't know what to expect. The first time we attempted this trail, our trip ended when we got to Two Harbors. We had read the maps and done our research, but ultimately, everything from Two Harbors forward was new territory.

We made our way back to the tarp tent, scanning the campsite with our headlamps and saying hi to all of the critters that had invited themselves to the sleepover.

"Good night, buddies!" Barry said as he switched off his headlamp.

I started to drift to sleep when I heard a scratching sound. I tapped Barry and asked him if he was awake. He was already reaching for his headlamp. He switched it on, and we spotted a fox approaching our makeshift tent.

Get it together, Williams. I thought to myself, recalling one of our playful mantras after some of my crying fits from the first day. I closed my eyes and told Barry to let me know when it was gone.

"Oh, he already scampered away, we're good. I don't think he'll be coming back."

"Don't think? If I wake up snuggling a fox, we're gonna have words, sir," I said, laughing through my fake rage.

"Don't say I never got ya nothin.'"

CHAPTER 15

EMBRACE YOUR STINK

I woke up in the cold the next morning and made tea to help warm myself up. After the sweaty cruise from the airport into Little Harbor, I was okay with a breeze and some clouds. As we packed up to head over to Two Harbors, I gave myself a wet wipe shower and put on more deodorant.

I went to the trashcan to toss the wipes and I still had the deodorant in my hand. I tossed the wipes and turned back toward our campsite. I took a few steps and stopped, looked back at the trashcan, then back at the campsite, then at the deodorant in my hand.

Did I need to bring deodorant on a backpacking trip? Turns out, it's a waste of space and pack weight, because after four days on a trail without a shower, you're going to start to smell. That's just how it goes. Even with my dip in the ocean on my birthday, I was still pretty ripe, thus the wipe down.

I started to walk back toward the trash can. I lifted the lid, then put it down.

This deodorant wasn't physically heavy. I had saved the end of my last tube of deodorant for this trip, so I didn't have to bring a full tube. So as far as adding weight to my backpack goes, it wasn't actually heavy. But emotionally? Woooo lord, this deodorant felt like an anvil in my hand. It was the same brand I tested on the first TCT hike, a product of beauty startup I eventually became CMO of for those 95 glorious days. This deodorant was loaded with emotional baggage, thus very heavy. This product was the first I tried that Molly made. When this all-natural deodorant kept me from smelling disgusting all the way across this trail the first time, I was officially a believer in the products she was making. When I got home from that first hike, I raved about the deodorant. I knew that personal care products were typically loaded with chemicals and I wanted to know more. If this deodorant was so great, what was the skincare line all about? I wanted to know everything. I had no idea back then that I'd ever work with her at that company, that I'd be CMO at that company, or that I'd quit after 95 days. I certainly didn't know that I'd be on the TCT two weeks after leaving the company, with nothing else in my way, no responsibilities other than safely hiking across this island.

On my first trip, I identified that I had been sold a bag of shit by the beauty industrial complex. I had spent my whole life trying to fit into a box, and on the trail the first time we attempted this hike, I found love for a body I didn't recognize. I had never felt that way about myself. On this trip, standing at this trash can with a tube of deodorant in my hand, the metaphors were almost too much to bear.

Still standing at the trashcan, I think about what this tube of deodorant represents to me on this trip. The end of a relationship. This deodorant no longer worked for me. I don't know if the formulation changed or if this was a rushed batch during the big orders, but I smelled to high heaven at home, let alone after four days and nearly 20 miles on the trail.

As if on cue, Barry comes cruising past with a wisdom drive-by:

"Hey, ditch the deodorant, embrace your stink," he said, cool as a cucumber.

As if I were now playing hot potato with this tube of deodorant, I picked up the lid and chucked the tube in the trash. I immediately felt lighter, like I did in the dressing room the first time, and after all the crying about my friends who had passed. Was this trashcan a portal? Was this deodorant actually weighing me down, spiritually and emotionally?

I raised my arm to smell my pits. *What died in here?*

"Embrace my stink? I'm so ripe!" I scoffed.

Then I thought about it. *Embrace my stink. Embrace my stink. The last time I focused on breaking down the myths I bought into about beauty standards, and on this trip, I'm chucking this deodorant in the trash, I don't need any of it. I'm going to embrace my stink!*

We all have a scent. Mine was unpleasant at that moment, but we all have a scent, it what makes us, us. What else makes me, me? What are the things that people have said are bad or wrong or gross about my body that I have been trying to fix for years, that I just physically cannot fix?

I looked at my thumbs.

I have brachydactyly type D. Better known as "clubbed thumbs" or as my sister liked to tease me, "toe thumbs." I didn't know anything was wrong with my thumbs until my sister jeered at me one day after school, "you know boys don't like girls with toe thumbs."

Sick burn.

For the rest of my adolescence, well into the seventh or eighth grade, I walked around with my thumbs tucked into my palm, forming a fist to hide the thumb. Kids being kids, sisters being the worst to each other, was this true? *Probably* not. Did I know that? Of course not. So, I hid my thumbs, hoping and praying that keeping them hidden would maybe give me a shot in hell at meeting a boy and making friends.

I looked at my thumbs as I went back to the picnic table to grab my gear and carry on to Two Harbors. I knew what was coming, we had a big climb out of this campground and then one of the huge sections with no switchbacks. This was going to be a brutal morning, but at least it wasn't sunny. The clouds would help us again today.

Me, moonlighting as my own hype man all the way up this ridge.

As we started hiking, I got a bit indignant about the thumb thing.

My thumbs are adorable.

Hey, when I give a thumbs up, it may be small and mighty, but there's no question that these are thumbs and they are up.

I found a boy who likes me. Wait. Has Barry seen my thumbs?

"Babe! Have you seen my thumbs?" I shout down to Barry.

He had me leading the way on this one and I was Betty-goating (lady version of being a billy goat) up this sucker. He couldn't hear me. I didn't want to repeat it, so I just flashed him a thumbs up.

He flashed one back.

I started crying.

I paused, got a sip of water, and took off my hat to wipe my forehead. I contemplated getting my cold towel out, but I knew we were climbing to one of the most gorgeous views on this hike, and the wind was already picking up. I let my hair blow around in the breeze, cooling my head down. As I ran my fingers through my hair to pull it back into a ponytail, my fingernail got snagged on a tangle.

I had a visceral reaction to the tangle and paused.

Where did that come from? I asked myself.

The last time my nails got stuck on my hair was when I got scolded for not straightening my hair for work.

It was the summer of 2010. I had just started skydiving and I was working at a prestigious PR firm in downtown Chicago. If you've seen Devil Wears Prada, it's like that, fashion-wise. The folks that worked there weren't nearly as vicious as the characters in the movie, but sometimes, the halls felt like a fashion runway. Coming from a suburb of Kansas City and this being my first job that wasn't in a restaurant, I had some catching up to do on all fronts related to business casual and corporate-appropriate makeup and hairstyles.

If you know me today, you know I wear my hair in its natural state. But prior to this section of the trail on this trip, I was a slave to a straightener for the better part of two decades. When I was working at the agency, the expectation was to look client-ready at all times. I was working in the Chicago office - one of the largest offices for this agency - and a lot of our clients were based in Chicago. You never knew who was in the building.

When I first started working there, I was making $10 per hour as an intern. When I got hired full time, I started earning $30k per year. Moving to a city where I didn't know anyone landed me in a studio apartment by myself. Add to that my monthly bus pass, paying back student loans, car insurance, groceries, and there wasn't much left at the end of the month.

Fashion had never been my priority. I was a cheerleader for most of my school years and wore our uniforms to school on game days, so I didn't need a lot of clothes. When I went to KU, I was on the rowing team and we had team gear that I wore to class most days, as most days we had two practice sessions between weights and conditioning and actual rowing practice. Didn't need a lot of clothes for college either.

So, this being my first job, not having a ton of money, I skirted the line of business casual and straight up casual more often than not.

When Barry and I started dating, I wanted to spend as much time at the drop zone as I could. I would drive to the office on Friday morning and pay to park in a lot like one of the senior executives did, all so I could get out to the drop zone on Friday after work. I rarely made it in time to get a jump in before sunset, but I didn't care, I just wanted to hang out with Barry after he got done working.

I'd spend all day Saturday and Sunday on the drop zone, jumping out of planes, helping where needed, chatting with Barry between jumps.

I'd spend the night Sunday night and then wake up Monday morning, shower and get ready at Barry's, then drive into the office, park at the garage, and go to work.

When I started pulling these longer weekends, I'd bring a bag with a change of clothes for work on Monday, my straightener and my makeup.

The drop zone was the first place I found since moving to Illinois where I felt like I could be me, fully expressed. I could wear my comfy athletic clothes and not be judged. I could shower and let my hair dry naturally, letting my natural waves and curls do what they do. I didn't wear makeup when I was jumping out of planes. I was just me. And it was glorious.

Until one weekend, I forgot my bag, and I didn't realize it until Monday morning. I went out to my car to grab my shower stuff and it wasn't there. No clothes. No shower stuff. No straightener.

Damnit.

Fortunately, both of Barry's roommates were quite social with the female skydiving students and licensed jumpers, so I was able to find some shampoo and conditioner in the bathroom. My hair wouldn't be straight, but I could wear it wavy and pull it back a bit to class it up. I could pull this off. I had the outfit I wore Friday. Fortunately, I changed for the bonfire, so it didn't smell of campfire and it was still clean. But Fridays are definitely super casual and the outfit I wore the previous Friday was very casual. It was all I had, and I would rather be on time and not totally client-ready than go all the way back to my apartment before work and end up being super late.

I got ready as best I could, kissed Barry goodbye, and went to the office. *I was early, good.*

Our office was in an old medical building and everyone except interns had their own office with a door.

I think I'm going to be okay. I thought as I passed her office.

The office I passed belonged to the woman who was my "assigned mentor" - someone I was paired with by HR when I made the transition from intern to full-time employee. Her role is to help me stay on track, keep an eye on my work, and make sure I'm abiding by company policy.

"Sydney?" she called out from her desk.

Shit shit shit shit shit. She saw me. I'm in trouble.

I walked to her office; head hung in shame like a kid on the way to the principal's office.

I knocked twice, she motioned for me to come in.

I sat down as she finished what she was typing.

She looked me up and down.

Yep, here it comes.

She wouldn't stop looking at my hair. I could feel my face getting hot with embarrassment as she turned back toward her computer screen.

"So, hi, good morning. How was your weekend?" she asked, not looking at me.

Jesus lady, let's get on with it already.

"It was great, I spent all weekend at the drop zone, which, by the way…"

She stopped typing and looked me up and down again. I trailed off as she gave me another once-over.

"We have clients in the building today."

Ah, agency-speak for *"what the hell are you wearing and why are you making me have this conversation with you?"*

"I know, I'm so sorry, it won't happen again."

"It just… Well, when you aren't client-ready, it looks unprofessional. We don't want to look unprofessional or unreliable."

"No, of course not, again, I'm super sorry."

She dismissed me and I went back to my office.

Okay, got it. If I want to stay gainfully employed this cannot happen again. God, I hope she doesn't tell my boss. I hope this doesn't turn into an Office Space situation where people keep coming up to me, asking me if I knew we have clients in the building.

Back on the trail, out of my daydream, I finish pulling my hair back, put my hat back on, and continue hiking.

Now, I envisioned myself as my own Flava-Flav, the hype man from Public Enemy back in the day. I was hyping myself all the way up. It worked with the thumbs thing, let's give it a go with the hair.

Nah girl, your hair is siiiiick. So many folks would spend good money to get texture like that. People buy products, get treatments, use devices to get hair like yours. And what, you woke up like that? Your hair is gorgeous and honestly, your hair has nothing to do with whether or not you're profession-al, or reliable. If ANYONE ever says that to you again, you don't need that negativity in your life - professionally or personally.

As I continued hiking, I heard my uncle Mike's voice.

Don't you dare cover up those tattoos, Sydney.

While I have several tattoos, I've always covered up. Paddleboarding helped me get over my irrational fear of people killing themselves at the sight of my exposed skin, but as far as my clothing choices were con-cerned, I was still hiding my arms and midsection. I thought about all the times I had covered up and was unnecessarily uncomfortable. Covering up because I wasn't confident in my own skin, I didn't want to be seen. I thought of all the invitations and opportunities I've turned down because I didn't want people to see me "like this" in my bigger body.

Standing on the Amtrak platform at Union Station in LA. July. Tempera-tures hovering around 95 degrees Fahrenheit. Trains throwing heat. Hair sticking to the back of my sweaty neck, sweat beading up on my upper lip. Probably 120+ degrees waiting for the train doors to open. Sweat dripping down my back. Oh god, can the people behind me see my sweat stains? On my way back to San Diego after spending three days in LA at the NBC offices. What am I wearing? A long sleeve shirt, black pants, ballet flats. Just trying to blend in.

I almost passed out that day while I was waiting for the train. I chose to be uncomfortably hot so I could be somewhat comfortable in public. As long as I wasn't being seen, life was good.

Thank goddess Barry recommended paddleboarding. That's done wonders for my confidence in my body.

I had lived in Southern California for seven years, and it wasn't until the summer of 2017 when I felt comfortable spending time in a swimsuit on the water. How many more memories could I have made? I didn't go to my high school reunion. I passed on opportunities that required nicer clothes because I didn't really have any.

I will never turn down another opportunity because I don't think I have time to lose weight before the event or because I don't feel fashionable enough.

I turned into my own hype man again, we were almost at the top.

Listen, your tattoos are sick. You paid good money for that art and you know you love them, don't hide them anymore. Let people see what you got!

It hit me. Three of my five tattoos were skydiving-related, or I got them at a skydiving event. The other two were memorial pieces. Yes, the art was great, yes, I wish my arms were more toned, but this wasn't only about my tattoos themselves or my discomfort in my body. Every tattoo I have starts a conversation. And until right now, on this side of this mountain, I wasn't ready to share the stories that correspond with each tattoo, because the memories themselves were too painful.

I went through my tattoos in order, reclaiming the stories of how and why I got them and why they were significant. I got my first tattoo the summer I started skydiving. One of Barry's students owned a tattoo shop, so he decided to host a tattoo party for his students in the city.

As I sat down, I knew what I wanted. Three closing pins in a circle, indicating the circle of life and the rule of threes. In skydiving, the number three comes up a lot. There are three handles you can pull. The first one is your main deployment handle which releases your main parachute. In the event of an emergency, if something is wrong with your main parachute, you pull a "cutaway" handle, which releases the parachute from your container (the "backpack" that skydivers wear), and then you pull your reserve handle, which deploys your reserve parachute. The system that keeps your parachute attached, before you choose to release it, is called a 3-ring, and it is made up of three rings that interlock together, which are easily released when the cutaway handle is pulled. The closing pin, of which I wanted three forming a circle, is a little curved piece of metal that fits through a loop of fabric that gets passed through several flaps of fabric to keep your skydiving container closed. When you're ready to deploy your parachute, you grab your deployment handle, throw it out into the airstream, and it catches air and extends a piece of webbing which is attached to the pin. The pin is extracted, and a few seconds later, you're floating through the sky under a fully functioning parachute.

The last anecdotes on the rule of threes - you try three times to correct a malfunctioning parachute before you cut it away, and when people die in skydiving, they tend to die in threes. When we would get word of one fatality, we'd hold our breath until the next two were announced, because it always seemed to happen in threes.

You've been covering this one since you got it, Sydney. Remember when you asked your account lead for permission to get a tattoo? Remember when you showed them what you got? Remember when you were interviewing for the agency in Austin and you were afraid you weren't going to get the job because of a tattoo on your wrist? You got this. You've always had this.

I got my second tattoo at the first big skydiving event I hosted in the sport. I hired the tattoo artist who did my tattoo the year prior to come out and set up shop in the skydiving classroom, making tattoos available for anyone who wanted one that day.

I wouldn't say that reading *Total Freedom* by Jiddhu Krishnamurti was a prerequisite for dating Barry, but it could have been. When we first started dating, he suggested I read it and I did. Borders Bookstore in downtown Chicago had the only print copy of this book in the city. I picked it up after work one day and dove straight in. It's a very heavy read - one of those books where you sit down, read a chapter, and then spend the next hour contemplating the meaning of life. The book changed how I see the world, helped me understand non-attachment, and gave me an inside look as to how Barry lived his life. He was so carefree and cool as a cucumber, despite working in what I would say is a high stress environment. This book showed me why.

A friend of mine had signed a copy of her book for me at a conference earlier that year, and I loved the way she wrote the letter F. I asked her if she could write out the phrase "total freedom" for me in her handwriting so I could get it tattooed on my foot. She sent me over a variety of options, and I picked one, printed it out, and brought it with me to the party.

I marched into the classroom where the artist was set up and handed him my piece of paper.

"I want this, on my foot, with stars on it."

He started sketching.

I thought my first tattoo was painful on my wrist. It was nothing compared to some of the areas on my foot. I was grimacing and forcing a smile and overall having a pretty tough time with this tattoo, but by the time it was done, I was in love.

I had the artist position the tattoo so I could read it when I looked down at my feet, versus having the words face the opposite direction, making it easier for other people to read. This tattoo was for me. Total Freedom was the title of the book, yes, but to get to this place, getting this tattoo, hosting this party, I took a lot of chances. I moved to Austin the fall after Barry and I met, then moved back to Illinois to work in skydiving. I took a chance on love with Barry and put my corporate career on hold. It was one of the best decisions I ever made. Total Freedom represented my freedom to choose. The placement on my foot was a reminder that I'm free to walk away from situations, people and jobs that were no longer serving my highest good.

Back on the trail, I thought to myself, *Total Freedom, huh? Am I psychic or did I just decide to really live my truth on this tattoo? When I got this back in 2011, I never would have guessed that I would have ended up living in Southern California, or that I would retire from skydiving, or that I'd be hiking up a mountain reclaiming these parts of my body that people said I should cover up if I ever wanted to maintain gainful employment. This tattoo is one of the ones I'm most proud of and I vow to share the story with anyone who asks.*

My first half-sleeve wasn't far behind. We returned to the same shop where I got my first tattoo for another tattoo party. By this time, I had been skydiving for over a year, and we were starting to think about where we were going to go for the winter. What were we going to do? This time, I wanted something that showed the balance between the sky and the water. A yin-yang of sorts. I knew by now to just come with a loose idea and to let the artist take the reins, and I'm so glad I did. It was a different artist this time, the one who had been doing Barry's tattoos. When he came back with the sketch, I was blown away.

It wasn't a literal circle-shaped yin yang, but the tattoo had a flow between the components that felt like yin and yang. On top, a bird with its wings fully extended, wearing a top hat. On the bottom, a koi fish splashing in the water. My balance between sky and water. Skydiving and Rowing, two decisions I had made for myself, by myself, that were pivotal parts of my life. I joked that I'd tell people I love eating chicken and sushi if I didn't want to get into the whole story.

I stopped to catch my breath, as I had been charging up this mountain at a good clip. I let the rest of the memory with my uncle play out in my head like a movie, letting his words ring loud and clear in my head. This was the tattoo my uncle loved so much. This is the one he told me not to cover up.

Don't you dare cover up those tattoos, Sydney.

Don't you dare cover up those tattoos, Sydney.

Don't you dare cover up those tattoos, Sydney.

I was wearing a shirt that covered up my tattoos, so I put my left hand on my right bicep and caressed it, petting the tattoo that lived underneath.

My next tattoo was a memorial piece for my grandmother. She loved stargazer lilies and butterflies. Those were my only two requirements. I don't remember how I found Outer Limits Tattoo in Long Beach, but the owner, Kari Barba was the one I wanted to have work on this tattoo. In researching the shop, we found out that not only was it the longest-running tattoo shop in North America, but that Kari was also the only tattoo artist, male or female, to enter a tattoo convention and win every category. She swept the thing! Her portfolio was incredible, and I was drawn to her energy. She was also $250 per hour. We weren't in Illinois anymore.

I remember when she showed me the sketch. In addition to the stargazer and butterflies, I requested a watercolor-style tattoo. In the research I had done online, in looking at photos of watercolor tattoos for inspiration, I would have been happy with the style I saw most commonly done; a gorgeous tattoo, with drips and drops of color here and there, as if someone were working with watercolors and accidentally dripped on your skin. What Kari came back with was a masterpiece. It looked like a literal watercolor painting, something that should be hung in a museum somewhere. It was hard to envision with the outline, but I trusted her and knew it was going to be magnificent.

I wasn't wrong. The piece took several sessions and I was obsessed with it. She managed to work depth of field into the art, the butterflies and part of the flower petal was in focus, the rest was blurred. There was a little pond beneath the flower, and it had a single drop creating a ripple in the water, with watercolor rainbow reflections on the surface of the water. There was so much nuance and detail.

I remember asking Kari if she ever felt energy during a tattoo session.

"Oh yes, of course" she responded, "I'm glad you asked because I feel it here, big time. Your grandmother was a sweet woman. I can feel her loving energy around this room, flowing through the machine, radiating from you. She is with you, always, both in spirit and now with this tattoo."

She handed me a small mirror to show me her progress. I gasped audibly, and felt tears welling up. I looked Kari in the eyes and mouthed *"thank you."* She nodded and went back to work.

The last tattoo I had done was a memorial tattoo for Adam.

I went back to Outer Limits, this time with Adam's mom and sister in tow. They were in town for his memorial skydive, which I was coordinating as a function of Planet Green Socks.

At the visitation following Adam's death, his mom and sister read a poem called "The Dash" by Linda Ellis. It talks about how on our tombstone, there is the day we were born and the day we die, and in between, that dash, is the life we live on this planet. The poem goes on to ask readers to reflect on how they live their dash. It was the perfect poem for Adam's funeral. He was only 23 when he died, but he lived a big life. He lived his dash. So, we were all three going to get "live your dash" on our forearm, with some kind of illustration that reminded us of Adam.

I didn't want standard tattoo script for this, I wanted real handwriting. A woman whom I had been working with on web design for the better part of a decade had really funky handwriting, so I asked her if she could write out "live your dash" for me to use in a tattoo design. Next to the words, I wanted a feather to represent Adam's eternal flight. He earned his wings now.

His mom chose a couple of elements from Adam's full-sleeve tattoo - a timer filled with sand, and a pair of dice. His sister got a compass, a reminder of his love of travel, and her desire to keep traveling in his memory.

We walked into the shop, introduced ourselves to the artist, and sat down to wait while she finished up the sketches. We spent all day in and out of that shop while we rotated through the chair. We shared memories and stories about Adam, and it was one of the most impactful days I had ever spent in a tattoo shop. Little signs of Adam were everywhere, and it brought me great comfort to know that his mom and sister were also tuned into his various appearances.

As the sun set and the tattoo shop got darker inside, I thought of one of Adam's signature phrases. On the drop zone in Illinois, we had the pleasure of witnessing some of the most beautiful sunsets over the corn fields. The land was so flat, and the sky was so vast, it really was a spectacular sight. Adam always used to say, *"you only get so many sunsets."*

By the time I got to the top of the peak, I felt incredible. I was out of breath, sweating like it was 100 degrees outside, and that process on the way up released some serious weight for me.

I took off my shirt. Now I was making up for lost time.

After reclaiming my shine up that ridge all morning, it was off with the shirt.

Sydney Williams doesn't wear shirts anymore. I thought to myself.

I asked Barry to take pictures of me on top of this peak. I put my hands on my hips, stood like a superhero, and took a few deep breaths. I took in the view while standing in my power for the first time.

I had just reclaimed parts of my body that people had told me I should fix. As I stood there, I recalled one of the lessons from the first hike – *I love my body*. On that first hike, I thought I was really loving my body, but here, in this moment, *this* feeling felt like self-love. What I had experienced on the first trip was the transition from hating my body to accepting it. That shift alone felt revolutionary for me because all of that negative self-talk takes up a lot of space, so in the absence of hatred, acceptance *feels* like love.

I didn't know if it was the TED talk about power posing, the exercise I had just done to reclaim my shine, or perhaps a combination of the two, but this right here felt like I was home – mind and body reconnected.

I took off my hat, walking to the edge of the cliff. I threw my arms up with glee, thanking this island for carrying the weight of the memories I was recounting here.

The wind picked up again and I let my hair down. It was tangled and matted after four days on the trail with no shower, and some of the natural texture was coming back. The wind whipped around my body, cooling me down rapidly on top of this peak. I scanned the surrounding area, observing the dramatic cliffs dropping into the ocean, looking back to where we came from, looking ahead to what was still in store for us on this section of trail.

This is new territory, I thought.

Geographically, everything after Two Harbors was new to us. Physically, I've never hiked this far in so many days. What will I feel like tomorrow? The day after that? What was Parsons going to be like? What about the route to get there? Emotionally, this is definitely new territory. I am working through some serious stuff so far on this trail, and while there has been a significant amount of crying, none of this is scary. None of this makes me sad. With each step, I feel more and more like myself. With each step, I feel like I'm getting closer to the woman I have always known I could be.

Confident that Barry got the shot, I turned around, made a beeline for my shirt and got dressed again. It was chilly up here, and I was really looking forward to getting into Two Harbors and grabbing a buffalo milk.

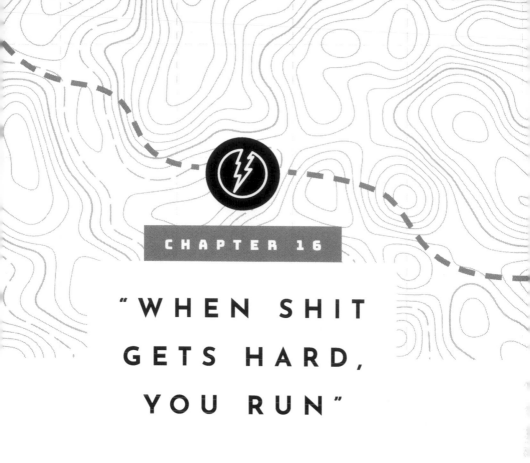

CHAPTER 16

"WHEN SHIT GETS HARD, YOU RUN"

As we continued hiking to Two Harbors, I kept thinking about what was coming up. I had read the maps and did my research, but I knew nothing about the last section of trail. The map we had with us showed elevation gain similar to that first day from Avalon to Blackjack, but it looked like it was just one big mountain versus up and down five peaks.

If we can find someone who's already hiked this section, that would be great, I thought.

As we got closer to town, Barry and I started chatting feverishly about the burger we had last time we were in Two Harbors.

"Was it really that good?" I asked. "I mean, we hiked 20-something miles to get here to get that burger. Do you think it's really the best burger we've ever had or was it just so good because it wasn't food in a bag?"

"Oh, I think it's that good. It was freaking Kobe beef for crying out loud. Those are happy cows!" Barry replied.

Everything about this stretch of trail felt like a trip down memory lane.

"This is where we had to wander through the fields because the road was so muddy!" Barry called out.

"This is where we got turned around and that nice couple asked us if we needed help!" I shouted as we made our way into town.

We made a beeline for the office on the dock where we would check in. This time, I knew where the campground was, and while I was sore, I wasn't completely incapable of making it another mile uphill. We checked in, got our key for our locker at Parsons the next day, and made our way up to the campsite.

We wandered through a group camp, a private campsite, and then onto the main campground. We were right by our own little cove. As we rolled up, the folks who were at the spot the night before were packing up. They had miniature cans of Diet Dr. Pepper and a couple bottles of Martinelli's apple juice – the good stuff.

"Do you guys want any of this?" one of them asked.

"Sure! Thanks!" we said, scooping up the cans and bottles to put them with our stuff.

We set up camp, our tarp and trekking poles serving as a makeshift tent again. We tucked our gear away in the tent and made our way down to the restaurant.

It was burger time.

Now that it was summer, the outdoor patio was open, so we snagged a table on the beach and waited for the server. I scanned the menu, as if I would order anything else than this burger. When the server came, we were more than ready.

"I'll have the Harbor Reef burger, onion rings, and a buffalo milk, please," I said.

The server looked at Barry.

"I'll have the exact same thing, thanks!"

We watched the waves roll in, watched hikers find their way to the office on the dock and then up to the campground. Our drinks arrived and we toasted to how far we had come, both literally across this island and in the grander sense; together as a couple, me managing diabetes and all of the changes along the way.

Shortly thereafter, our burgers arrived. I could smell them before I could see our server.

That first bite was just as magical as it was on the last trip. Eye roll inducing. I cannot confirm or deny, but there may have been a slight moan.

As much as I would have loved to savor every single bite, that wasn't happening, my hiker hunger had taken over. We inhaled the burgers and rings, agreeing that the burger was even better than we remembered it being, and ordered another buffalo milk for dessert. After I ordered, I paused and started doing the math around calories and blood sugar, considering if I could really "afford" to have a second buffalo milk.

I had just hiked 26 miles across this trail. My blood sugar was spectacular so far. Historically, my relationship with food was so chaotic, but Diabetes gave me permission to finally take control of my life, no excuses. I didn't want this buffalo milk to be the thing that made me slide back to 200+ pounds with blood sugar through the roof.

Get it together, Sydney. Listen to your body. If you want another buffalo milk, have one, but don't beat yourself up about it. You're doing great.

I snapped out of my shame spiral. Damn straight, I could make healthy choices. And damn straight I had the discipline and desire to keep Diabetes at bay. End of story.

I enjoyed a second buffalo milk and then we walked back to the campsite. We met a couple along the way who was doing the trail in reverse.

Ask and the Universe provides, I thought.

This couple had just completed the loop out to Parsons and was settling into Two Harbors today before continuing on toward Little Harbor tomorrow.

I asked them what the route to Parsons Landing was like and they confirmed my understanding.

There were two routes out to the last campground. If you wanted to follow the trail in sequential order, then the route out of Two Harbors was challenging. Yes, it was similar to the first day on trail, yes that elevation gain was done in one fell swoop, and no, there weren't many switchbacks. It was all uphill, all day. And then of course, what goes up must come down. The descent into Parsons Landing was very steep, and the terrain was that loose gravelly stuff, so have your poles ready, watch your step, take your time, and hike your own hike. The return route out of Parsons Landing back to Two Harbors, the section they just completed, was a nice flat fire access road that hugs the coastline. It's like your victory lap to end the trip, no real elevation gains to worry about, just gorgeous views of all the little coves along the way.

I thanked them for the intel, and they split off to go to their campsite. Barry asked me which way I wanted to go in the morning. Knowing I can do hard things, one of the lessons I learned on the first trip, I wanted to go the hard way. Get it over with. If we had enough energy to keep going out to Starlight beach, we could do that too.

When we got back to the campsite, I busted out my little notebook. The hike from Little Harbor was pretty powerful and I wanted to remember what I experienced there.

TCT JOURNAL ENTRY

JUNE 5, 2018
Little Harbor to Two Harbors
Steps: 23,493
NOTES ON TRAIL: looks like they changed the trail a bit up front, the pink/white rock scramble wasn't part of this section anymore.

BIGGEST WINS:

✓ this time wasn't muddy!
✓ burger + buffalo milk for lunch
✓ blood sugar seems to be regulating itself at this point

LESSONS LEARNED:

✓ Last time, I tested probiotic deodorant and realized I didn't need the products/lies the beauty industrial complex has been selling. This time, I ditched the deodorant and realized I didn't need any of it.
✓ "Embrace my stink," – my stink is the literal stink on the trail, it's also the things that make me ME, so I don't need to change myself, the "way I smell" is just fine and doesn't need to be masked – THIS IS BIGGER THAN PITS.

MAJOR THEMES SO FAR:

✓ Embrace my stink
✓ My stories are mine to tell – embrace my newness. I have a gift for communicating with newbies.
✓ How did we get ready for the TCT? What steps did I take mentally?
✓ Big changes from 2016 to now
✓ no two hikes are the same

- ✓ hike your own hike – it's not a race
- ✓ stripping shit away – pack weight and life weight
- ✓ you don't really need a lot to survive
- ✓ survival in the outdoors is all about improvisation

WHAT AM I THANKFUL FOR?

- ✓ currently thankful for this vest, best new purchase for this trip
- ✓ overall, I continue to be grateful for how well I'm managing this disease
- ✓ again, realizing how much I love Barry and how far we've come

HOW AM I FEELING RIGHT NOW?

- ✓ Physically: 100%. one small blister on right toe, but all good otherwise
- ✓ Mentally: strong AF and ready to tackle the leg to Parsons tomorrow
- ✓ Emotionally: I feel this weird combination of empty and full. Which feels like I've made the space for what's next.
- ✓ Overall: I realized in the tent that I have the ability to grant myself the permission I've been seeking. I felt weird during my last video journal and it's because I knew this was coming. I just needed to get through my realization. I already feel more at home with myself.

NOTE:

Prejudice against ourselves. We keep saying we don't know how we survived this trip the last time and it's not some big mystery – we are hustlers. Last time we were the least physically fit we've ever been, period. This time, I'm in the best shape I have ever been in.

We called it an early night and fell asleep to the sound of waves lapping at the rocks below our campsite. When I woke up, Barry said he wanted to get breakfast in town, so we packed up and headed to the restaurant. I ordered a bagel with smoked salmon and Barry got a breakfast sandwich. We sat down outside and enjoyed our breakfast as the rest of the hikers started to wake up. As we finished our breakfast, we saw another couple donning big backpacks heading toward the start of the loop to Parsons. Following suit, we packed up and started making our way back to the trail.

As we started climbing out of the harbor toward the ridgeline, I heard a voice pop into my head:

"When shit gets hard, you run."

I had been hearing this off and on throughout this hike and in the weeks preceding it. I was hoping I could just hike it out, but like I said in my journal entry before this trip, I can't bypass the talking it out part. So up this mountain, I talked it out. With myself.

When shit gets hard, you run. I thought. The first time I heard it, it sounded like my voice in my head. As if I were saying this to myself.

Remembering back to when I was in the dressing room the first time - would I talk to myself like that? No. I thought back to some of the prior meditations I had exercised about releasing people, situations, behaviors, and habits that no longer serve me.

What would it feel like to let that go? I wondered.

As I kept hiking up to one of the highest points on the island, I imagined weight being lifted off my shoulders as I released the power I gave that phrase. I felt lighter and my pace quickened.

After a while, it came back into my head. *"When shit gets hard, you run."*

This time, it didn't sound like my inner voice. It sounded like my former business partner. I could see the way her head would move when she said that to my face. The flash of disgust in her eyes, as if I were a problem to be fixed when I had a panic attack in her living room. I imagined more weight being lifted, letting go of that phrase again. I didn't feel lighter. It felt like I was stuck in this emotion, this loop, like this was a CD and it was skipping on this one phrase. Recalling how I felt at the top of one of the peaks yesterday after being my own hype man up that really tough climb on the ridgeline, I thought about how I might pump myself up here. Thinking back to that dressing room, when I was talking to myself like I would speak to my best friend, I tried it from that place. What would Kat tell me if she was trying to pump me up in this situation?

Okay, Sydney, listen, you've jumped out of an airplane nearly 700 times, that's hard.

And you've moved all over this country for love and work. Find a thing, uproot your life, land somewhere else. Multiple times. Even if you like doing it, transplanting again and again is a lot. I'd say that's hard.

Ooh, and you're coming up on 30 miles hiked across this island. That's hard, too!

I stopped to catch my breath. I felt lighter, and I was crying. I was so happy and feeling so floaty I didn't even realize I was crying. I couldn't make sense of it. This was one of the steepest parts of the island and I was cruising. Where was this energy coming from? I kept hiking, feeling more energized than I had since we first got on this trail five days ago. We came up to a flat break before turning further toward the interior of the island. I asked Barry to record me. I was ready to do an interview.

"The last time I was doing this, I didn't know that I could, so with every step, I was proving myself wrong. This trip, I knew I could, and with every step, I'm proving myself right. I'd guess we are about halfway up, elevation wise, and I feel incredible. I feel so healthy. We'll show you what it looks like when we get to Parsons."

I flashed the camera the biggest thumbs up.

We had a considerable distance to cover so we kept moving, and as we did, more thoughts bubbled up to the surface. More one-liners that had stuck with me and become my internal soundtrack, my negative self-talk, ready to take me down the second I felt too confident.

"Watch out for her wrath, she's violent."

Hmm, I don't like that.

I imagined what it would feel like to let that go, feeling the weight lift off my shoulders. Like before, the voice came back, and this time, it wasn't mine. It was my sister. She said my reactions were explosive and unpredictable, that I had a certain wrath I would throw in anyone's direction when I was in that state. She wasn't compassionate in this description; she wasn't trying to understand why I might be having that kind of reaction. She was judging. I thought about this phrase. Was I violent, truly? Was I honestly a violent person? No, of course not. Did I have big reactions sometimes? Yes, I definitely did. Where did those reactions come from? I thought back to a time where she called me on it. If I were in a similar situation, right now in this grounded state, would I have the same response? Is that how I'd want to show up? No? Okay then let's dig for the root of that reaction. Was it mine? Was this something I internalized that I could unlearn?

I kept hiking, and continued the exercise:

Okay, Sydney, you're definitely not violent. Are you kidding me? The girl that talks to flowers and hugs trees? Not violent.

Also, the second you started standing up for yourself, all of the sudden she says you're violent? Sounds like she was uncomfortable with you having boundaries and wanted to keep you small.

Listen, you didn't know what you didn't know. Now that you know that there is a difference between reactions and responses, and now that you know some of your triggers, you can handle these kinds of things better moving forward.

Also, you're not your dad. Quit taking on his reactions as your own.

I stopped dead in my tracks and put my hands on my knees. This felt like another exorcism of sorts. Keeled over, scream-crying at the ground, tears freefalling to the dusty trail between my feet. It felt like it did the other day - warm, bright, light and floaty. Did I die… again?

I opened my eyes and the sun had peeked through the clouds.

Okay, earth goddess warrior hiker chick, take it easy. I mocked myself.

We kept hiking, and this process repeated over and over, with more of these one-liners. And every time, I repeated the process. This was a long slog of a hike; I had a lot of time to sort through it.

Here are some of the other negative bits that came up for me while we climbed toward Silver Peak:

You're too fat.

You're too loud.

You're too short to row on the Varsity team.

Big girls, like you, will never be a flyer in a cheerleading stunt, you'll always be a base.

Could you bring your first date personality to this client meeting?

If you want to make friends here, I suggest you tone down your enthusiasm.

You're too young to do that.

Every drop zone has a bicycle. This season, you're the bicycle - everyone gets a ride. You're such a slut.

If it's not her idea, she'll shut it down.

If you give her enough leash on this project, she'll hang herself, just watch.

Nobody will ever love you.

You're such a bitch.

Are you sure you're stable enough to do this?

I could fuck him while you're gone.

You are disgusting, I can't believe I slept with you.

I saw a path to a higher viewpoint and turned toward it, sprinting up the hill to get to the view. By the time I got to the top, I was out of breath, gasping for air. I had my hands on my head, trying to catch my breath and slow my heart down. I turned toward the ocean and stood there, looking out at the view while Barry made his way up to me. My whole body was vibrating. I asked Barry to take a picture of me. There wasn't a lot of room where we were, so I took up most of the frame. It wasn't the perspective I was looking for, but we didn't have many options. I posed, with my arms up, feeling electric. Not on fire, not uncomfortable, just hyper-aware of my body, and what it felt like to be alive. I was still trying to slow my breathing and take long, deep breaths. I could feel my lungs and my belly rise with the inhales, and felt my whole body relax on the exhale. My legs were twitching a little bit from the sprint up the hill. I felt sweat beading up under my lip, on the back of my neck, and between my breasts. My body was working. I could feel all of it. It was otherworldly.

Feeling electric at the top of this viewpoint.

This feeling was familiar, but different. There was another couple behind us and they joined us at the viewpoint. Perfect, I could actually get a picture of me and Barry.

We scooted back as far as we could, hoping maybe they'd have better luck with getting more of the scenery in frame. The sun was coming out and I was so excited to have photos of this side of the island without an overcast sky.

While they tried to get different angles, I was holding a smile and thinking to myself;

When was the last time I felt this good? When was the last time I felt this supported by the people in my life? When was the last time I felt this confident in the direction my life is going? When was the last time I felt this connected to my body, this comfortable in my own skin? When was the last time I felt this capable?

I popped a few electrolyte chews to keep my energy up on the descent into the Parsons Landing campground. The couple behind us hiked with us for a bit, and they said they were headed out to Starlight Beach. I wanted to hike out to Starlight, but if this downhill was anything like what the folks described yesterday, I just wanted to get down to Parsons safely and enjoy the last campground for as long as we could.

We split at the fork for Starlight and turned towards Parsons Landing.

CHAPTER 17

IT'S ALL GOODE

They weren't kidding, this section of the trail was steep. My legs were exhausted from the climb to the top, my body was energized after feeling so alive once we got there, and my mind was seeking answers. I repeated the questions again in my mind.

When was the last time I felt this good? When was the last time I felt this supported by the people in my life? When was the last time I felt this confident in the direction my life is going? When was the last time I felt this connected to my body, this comfortable in my own skin? When was the last time I felt this capable?

Barry was pretty far ahead of me and I felt myself moving faster than I wanted to. I paused and dug in my poles. I closed my eyes and took a deep breath.

Hike your own hike.

I exhaled, opened my eyes, and started hiking again, this time taking smaller steps, using more caution, paying attention to where I was going. As long as I kept looking at my feet, I couldn't freak out about how steep this part of the trail was and how loose the ground was.

I thought about the times I felt comfortable in my body, before this trip.

2016: After we did the first hike.

2013: The first year I went to Nationals.

2011: When I was running when we lived on the drop zone in Illinois.

Comfortable in my body was a bit of a stretch. At those points, I didn't *hate* my body, but it was nothing close to this. I was at varying stages of indifferent, with that first hike being the catalyst that launched this journey I'm on right now. That's different from *this* feeling. When was the last time I felt like *this*?

I kept my head down, as if the answer would be written in the loose gravel and dirt. Seeking. Looking for answers in this trail the same way I used to pray they'd be written at the bottom of a pint of Ben & Jerry's or at the bottom of the wine bottle.

When was the last time I felt this good?

Pleading with the Universe, God, angels, whatever you believe in. *What is it? When was it?*

I picked my head up to see where Barry was, and my foot started to slide out from under me. I dug in my poles, caught myself, and redistributed my weight. I took a deep breath and closed my eyes.

The last time I felt this good, this supported, this comfortable in my skin, this confident in the direction my life is going, this connected to my body, this capable - was right before I was raped 12 years ago.

Standing, panting, braced as if I were traversing the gates of a downhill ski run, everything started to make sense. My pulse quickened; my mind was racing. If this were a cartoon, it would have sounded like a slot machine in my head. All of the chaotic parts of my life over the last 12 years were arranging themselves, and these fragmented parts of my life since the assault started to come into alignment. *This* was the missing puzzle piece.

If my brain were a computer, the only way I can describe what happened next was like downloading a massive folder of files on the fastest internet connection you can imagine and seeing flashes as it's being downloaded. It felt like every movie sequence I'd ever seen of someone's life flashing before their eyes. I thought maybe I had fallen down and hit my head, and this was a dream, but it wasn't. I was on the trail. Standing, leaning into my trekking poles, looking down at Parsons Landing, Barry now far away in the distance. I was flooded with flashbacks from relationships, moments in classrooms, questionable decisions, arguments with people I loved, and reactions to things people have said to me over the years.

When I connected these dots, I wasn't scared, and I wasn't sad. I felt free. For the first time in my life, everything that felt out of character or chaotic or out of my control made sense. We still had quite a distance to go to get down to the campground. I shook my head, shook my hands out, and looked around. I wanted to take all of this in. I took some photos of where I was when I had this revelation, knowing this was one of the most important moments of my life. While I was looking through the screen at the landscape ahead of me, I saw a hat hanging on a fence post.

I tucked my camera back in my pocket and got a grip on my poles and side-stepped down the trail to get to the fence post. It was a cream-colored dad hat with white stitching proclaiming "It's All Goode". *What's with the E?* I got my phone out again and took a picture of the hat. What the hell?

You see a hat, I see a sign from the Universe.

I looked around, wondering if I was actually Truman Burbank (Jim Carrey's character from "The Truman Show") and this was my movie set. *Is someone messing with me?* I felt goosebumps head to toe and started crying. Not sad tears. Joy. Tears of pure joy. I was home. In my body. On this trail. With Barry. I had more confidence now, and I didn't feel like I had to take itty bitty baby steps. I took normal steps. This was steep, but it was starting to level out. As it did, I started skipping.

I thought about the bikini photoshoot I wanted to do with Barry in Little Harbor that I ended up doing myself. I was disappointed that I didn't ask him to take pictures that day because the next day was overcast and didn't highlight Little Harbor in the same way. Overcast did not match how sunshiny I felt there. I had been through a lot between then and now.

The thumbs? Hair? That whole big long list of horrible shit that I had internalized? No wonder I felt so amazing - I just let go of A LOT of stuff.

Bikini pictures didn't feel like enough. I wanted to run into the water, fully naked. I wanted to give myself this gift. For the first time in a long time, I was at home in my body and I knew why I wasn't before. I wanted documentation of me feeling this embodied. Plus, when I'm old and gray, and things are hanging in different places, I want to remember how powerful my body has been, how powerful it *always* has been, at every stage of my life.

I shouted ahead to Barry.

"Hey, when we get down there, I want to take off all my clothes and run into the ocean. I love my body, and I want pictures of me doing this, will you be my cameraman?"

Barry stopped and turned around. The sun was behind me and shining in his eyes, so he lifted his arms to shield his face so he could see me.

"Hell yeah I'll be your cameraman!" he shouted back.

We still had a few miles to go to get down to the campsite, and as I continued down the mountain, I wondered what I just committed to.

Goodness, I just started taking my shirt off, now I'm getting naked? Who am I? What did I just sign up for?

We made our way down the trail, connected with a road into the campground, and scoped the place out. We found our locker, grabbed the water and firewood we ordered, and walked over to our campsite.

"This beach just took over as my favorite place to camp on this island, if not in the world," I said.

We found our campsite, the last one on the left side of the lockers. We had the whole corner of this beach to ourselves, hell, we had this whole beach to ourselves. There wasn't a soul in sight.

We put our water in the fox box and left our bags out on the bench of the picnic table. I was really looking forward to enjoying that cookie after this little rebirth ceremony.

I unpacked my DSLR and handed it to Barry. I took off all of my clothes, took off my hat and let my hair down, tucking my ponytail holder in my bag. I took off my rings, watch, and bracelet. The only thing that was on me that wasn't mine was my contact lenses. Since there was nobody else on this beach, I didn't grab my towel to take with me down to the water, I just marched my happy naked ass from the picnic table to the waves, free as a bird.

Barry followed me with the camera, clicking away.

I got to the ocean and paused. I looked around at the crystal-clear water, bright blue skies, and a bunch of seagulls pecking at the sand to my right. I started to walk into the waves, and by the time I was knee-deep, I knew I was going to have to make this quick. This water was coooold. I had fallen off my board a few times last year, but other than that, I hadn't spent much time in the ocean, so this was a surprise. I fully expected this to feel like the Caribbean. Nope. I waded out a bit further, about up to mid-thigh. I let a few waves crash against my body, trying to reduce the shock as I walked out deeper. As the water went up to my belly button, a wave crashed and hit my butt, soaking me up to the tops of my shoulders.

Yep, far enough. I thought as I licked my lips, tasting the salty seawater as I did.

I threw my arms up.

Hey, so I don't know what's up on this island, but this has been a pretty spiritual experience, I thought to myself, halfway talking to the Universe, God, or whoever else might be listening. At this point I didn't know what was going on, just that I was uncovering something big.

And if there's anything else for me to learn here, I'm open to it. I'm ready to receive it. As soon as I said "receive it" I laughed to myself. I remembered how hard I was dry heaving by the end of that women's retreat when the speakers kept talking about manifesting your best life and abundance and being willing to receive.

Fuck me, I cannot believe I'm saying this shit. But if there's a shot in hell it works, then it's worth saying: Thank you, thank you, thank you, thank you. Whatever this was, I am so grateful for this experience, and I promise I'll do whatever it takes to keep learning and growing.

I lowered my arms, turn around, and looked back at Barry. He was still taking pictures. I turned back toward the ocean, ready to start my dunking process. My mission is to get this picture of me like Ariel from "The Little Mermaid" - where she majestically emerges from the ocean onto that rock. I took a deep breath, plugged my nose, and started to lower myself underwater. I dropped down to get my head under water, bumping my butt on the ocean floor. I hadn't walked out far enough. It was too cold. The abrupt stop to my dunking maneuver startled me, and I started this little limbo move as I ducked down to get my whole self under the water, further committing to the Ariel shot. I repositioned my feet to get stable, popping back up to standing in waist-high water. I rubbed the saltwater out of my eyes and smoothed my hair back.

When I opened my eyes, everything seemed a bit sharper. The colors were more vibrant, as if someone had dehazed my field of vision.

As I looked out to the ocean in front of me, I knew that I had been hiking my feelings, that much was abundantly clear. But in this moment, in this water, and at those pivotal points along this second hike, I was reclaiming my body. Reclaiming it from the people who said it wasn't good enough, or that it needed to be fixed to fit in a very narrow standard of beauty, and from the man who assaulted it. I had been rebirthed.

Hiking my feelings. Reclaiming my body.

I walked back toward Barry with the biggest smile on my face.

The next day was our victory lap back to Two Harbors, following a flat gravel road that hugged the coastline. I had seven miles to go to finish this trail. It was happening.

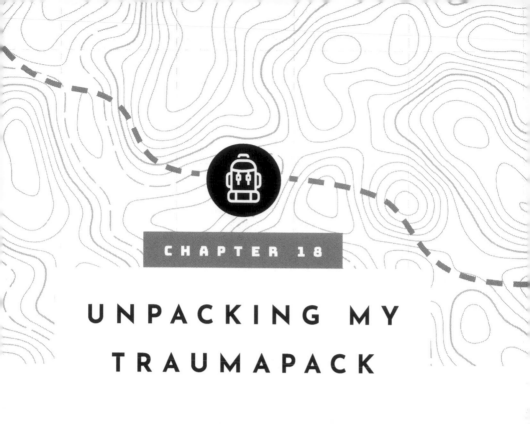

CHAPTER 18

UNPACKING MY TRAUMAPACK

T he sunset after my rebirth ceremony was incredible. That night, we sat by the campfire and watched for shooting stars. We didn't set up our tarp, we decided to cowboy camp on the beach. The waves lapping on the rocks were the perfect white noise to ease me into one of the best nights of sleep I had gotten in over a decade, since the assault. I was safe. Happy. Free. Loved.

The next morning, we woke up and it was overcast again. As we packed up camp, I didn't want to leave.

Can we stay here? I could live here. I've got everything I need, and I could just go back and forth to Two Harbors every few days to stock up on snacks and supplies.

When I grabbed my backpack to sling it over my shoulder, I felt like Hulk. The backpack felt as if there were nothing in it. On a literal level, we had eaten all of the food we came with, so our packs were significantly lighter than they were the first day. I started thinking about everything I worked through all over this island, and as we made our way out of Parsons Landing back to the trail, I found a bit more understanding. After my rebirth ceremony, I realized that I've been hiking through life with this invisible backpack on, full of my trauma.

Trauma Pack. A backpack full of trauma. That's the one I was emptying here.

The chaos that had occurred in my mind and body since the assault was the first thing to click for me. As we made our way back to Two Harbors, I thought back to Chemistry 101 the semester after the assault. I was on track to go to medical school, but I was failing Chem 101 and had to drop the class to save my GPA. When I kept failing tests and was completely unable to retain the information, I thought it was because I was dumb. I berated myself.

Who the hell do you think you are? You can't even pass Chem 101. How are you going to get into the higher-level science classes? How are you going to get into medical school?

I didn't seek help, I didn't think to explore this sudden change in academic performance, I just thought I was suddenly dumb, incapable of completing this science class, and I followed that belief all the way. Not only did I drop the class, I changed my course of study entirely. I asked myself what I liked doing and what I was good at, looking for the lowest hanging fruit, something I could pivot to that would be easy for me.

At the time, I was bartending to pay for school, and I was really good at upselling. I also loved sharing stories with my bar regulars. Storytelling and selling - that's what felt natural to me. So, I changed my plan and applied to the School of Mass Communications at the University of South Florida. I picked the public relations track and did my senior project on digital and emerging media. I succeeded in this course of study and went on to have a great career, but the impetus for the change wasn't because I was stupid, not by a long shot.

Looking back, my studies suffered because I was in a state of unresolved trauma. I didn't get help after the assault and I was not equipped to heal myself. I didn't know how badly I was hurting; I didn't realize what a heavy load I was carrying. Even though I couldn't wrap my head around what had happened to me, my body knew. And my body protected itself.

My unresolved trauma required numbing to keep it hidden and buried, so I developed coping mechanisms like eating and drinking to find comfort or to numb the pain.

"Why was I eating or drinking my feelings to begin with?"

There it was. That early childhood conversation with my mom was the root of my body image issues, the rape caused the coping mechanisms, and I could see how they compounded and how things got out of control as I suffered loss after loss during the years where it felt like everyone around me was dying.

I had lost 60 pounds since I was diagnosed with Diabetes, and it was easy. Now the ease made sense. For my entire life, I thought that once I got to Destination Hot Body, I would find happiness. It wasn't until I started doing some mindset work around my disordered relationship with food that I was able to connect the dots.

For most of my life, food was the adventure. Food was the feeling. Food was how I expressed love. Food was how I soothed myself through the hardest years of my life. For me to manage my diabetes effectively, I had to change my mindset around how I nourished myself. If my go-to coping mechanisms were eating and drinking my feelings, and if I wanted to be the best diabetes patient my doctor had ever seen, I knew I couldn't keep digging into a pint of ice cream or polishing off a bottle of wine when I needed comfort.

Once I identified why I was using food as an emotional crutch, I was able to shift my mindset. Now, food was the *fuel* for the adventures that I wanted my body to be able to enjoy.

Now it was clear to me; when my mental health improved, my physical health followed. Happiness was never waiting for me on the other side of the perfect body, it was a byproduct of taking care of myself – mentally, physically, spiritually. Doing *that* led me to joy, peace, and happiness.

This outlet of Hiking My Feelings sped up the process for me, because I couldn't run away or numb what was coming up for me when I was in the middle of the backcountry. *Right foot, left foot* was a mantra I used to drag my legs up the mountain on the first day, but it has also carried over into my life off the trail. As I figure out how to start our non-profit and raise money for our retreat center, I have to keep going. I can't just give up. On the trail, I couldn't just stop hiking, we had to keep moving, even when it hurts, to get to our next destination. In life, it is the same way. When it hurts, when it gets hard, I can't give up.

I had tried to lose weight by going to the gym, but it didn't work for me. And let's be honest, most gyms aren't designed for true holistic wellness of the mind, body, and soul. Between the beefcakes dropping weights, the news blasting on the TVs telling you how the world is melting down and commercials telling you which drugs you need for your condition or which products you should buy to improve your life, it's not exactly a positive, vibrant environment.

Now that I was starting to understand how the trauma affected my mind and body, the metaphor of the backpack made so much more sense. There were a handful of pivotal moments on the trail for me, and if we're using the metaphor of our trauma being these items in the backpack, let's talk about what I unpacked on this island.

The first big piece of trauma I pulled out was the grief that I hadn't processed for my friends who had passed. I held that grief in my hands, gave it the attention it deserved, and didn't put it back in my backpack. What I put back in my pack was positive memories, their legacy, and my commitment to sharing their stories whenever I could to keep their spirits alive. Underneath that heavy stuff, I was able to take off my shirt at that playground in the middle of nowhere, choosing to cool down naturally versus being unnecessarily uncomfortable yet again.

As I marched up one of the ridgelines between Little Harbor and Two Harbors, I was pulling out more heavy items, things people had said I should change about my body that I physically can't or was tired of trying to fix. I reclaimed my thumbs, my hair, and my tattoos. When I got done exploring that trauma, I replaced it with the positive things I said to myself, lightening the backpack once again. And in return, at the top, I felt powerful in my body for the first time.

And on the way toward Silver Peak, the hard route from Two Harbors to Parsons Landing, I realized just how much of the stuff in the backpack wasn't mine. The things that came up for me there first came into my head as my voice, my inner critic. Every time I heard my voice, I stopped myself.

We don't talk like that around here, I thought to myself. *And what would it feel like to let it go?*

Once I released those thoughts and vowed to never speak to myself like that again, when these thoughts came back around, it was the voice of who actually said it. In those moments, I knew that these things weren't mine. They were other people's fears, insecurities, and projections. Since they were said to me by folks who were super important to me, whose words I treated as The Truth without question - family members, coaches, mentors, bosses, select friends and colleagues - I internalized those comments as *my* truth. Or, they were said to me or about me enough times that I figured if someone wanted to take that much time out of their day to say these things, they must be true.

I'm a kind woman, but I don't need to carry people's heavy stuff for them anymore.

By the time I got to the top of that peak, I had tossed so much of this stuff that wasn't serving me of my bag and replaced it with more love for myself, more compassion, more permission to continue to release these things as they come up for me.

Underneath all of the lies I had been feeding myself, I found the biggest, heaviest piece of trauma in my pack; the sexual assault. Once I cleared the way to get to my ooey gooey center, my deepest darkest secret, it wasn't so scary. I had so much practice speaking kindly to myself that by the time I got down to the sexual assault at the bottom of the traumapack, hanging out in there like a cinder block, there was no way that discovery was going to take me down. Very quickly, that piece of trauma became the brightest light, and the biggest source of understanding, love, compassion, and empathy for myself and everything that happened in my life - good, bad or indifferent - since the assault. It was only heavy when I didn't know what it was. I didn't see it until I was ready. And by the time I did, I knew what to do and how to handle it.

PRO-TIP: People don't like it when you give them their heavy items back. They gave it to you for a reason. Once those words don't control your every move, the folks who gave them to you will not be happy for you. They want you to be miserable too, and they want you to pass it on like the common cold. It is your duty to yourself to break the cycle.

When you're in a constant state of trauma, constantly triggered, feeling fight or flight about everything, your hormones do wild things. Your cells become inflamed, and then your body retains weight. My coping mechanisms were bringing more disease upon a body that already didn't feel safe existing in public.

Even when I thought I was totally fine in the years that have passed during the assault, I had that secret eating away at me. The outbursts my sister referenced made sense. I still wouldn't classify them as violent in any way, but the out of character reactions had context now. I didn't know what was being triggered, everything just felt out of control. I thrived in environments that required all of my attention. At first, that was my career. I wanted to get control of myself and my situation. I wanted to be able to provide for myself. I didn't want to have to rely on a partner for support. So, I jumped into a career. I took on extra assignments and was happy to be the first person in, the last person out. And I was rewarded heavily for my "work ethic" - promotions, raises, and unique opportunities considering how junior I was.

Between my people-pleasing tendencies and ignoring the trauma, I was a pressure cooker. Everyone else came first, and on the rare occasion I would put my needs first and get called selfish as a result, I had a visceral reaction to it, and dug my heels in further on neglecting my needs. I showed up for everyone always but couldn't ever show up for myself. Not surprisingly, this behavior got me places too. Being available for everyone all the time is a great way to get invited to brainstorms, exposure to senior leadership, and face time with clients. It also rolls out the red carpet for emotional, physical, and spiritual burnout.

As I earned more responsibility, my death grip on my life tightened even more. As more and more people relied on me, I was harder and harder on myself. I was almost crushed by the weight of the impossible expectations I had set for my life. At the same time, it was impossible for me to see further than a year or two into the future. It was scary to make plans since mine were so violently ripped out from under me.

I heard Barry up ahead of me and came back into my body, shifting out of dot-connecting mode. Even though this last day on the trail was flat, I was exhausted. My brain was doing most of the work, connecting the dots from all of the seemingly unrelated events that had occurred since the assault, and over the course of our two hikes across the island. It really did feel like a victory lap, and as we passed mile marker 33 of the Trans-Catalina Trail, I paused and cried. This was the mile marker I was most looking forward to on this trail – celebrating the farthest I had ever hiked, my 33rd birthday, and a new commitment to myself from this trip moving forward.

I did it. I knew I could do it. And if I could do *this*, what else was possible?

For the last five miles, I skipped and cried as we made our way back into the town of Two Harbors. I wanted to sprint because I was so excited, and I wanted to stop and sit down because I didn't want this experience to end.

Barry and I stopped right before the last turn into town and hugged.

"I'm proud of you," he said one last time, hands on my face. He pulled me in for a kiss.

I sniffled so my boogers wouldn't interfere with the kiss.

"I'm proud of me, too." I whimpered through my tears.

While I knew I had learned a lot about myself on this trip, I also knew there was a lot of work ahead of me. This was a big step in my healing journey, and I knew it wasn't the last.

EPILOGUE

What do I wish I knew when I was younger? What kind of support or advice do I wish I had after my assault? And how are all of these different events related? If I could leave you with three takeaways from my experience, here's what I'd say:

GET HELP, TREAT THE WOUND.

Trauma is not a scratch; it is an open wound. If I were next to you while you were reading this with a compound fracture on my arm – bone out of the skin – you would put down the book and get help, maybe even take me to the hospital. If I were bleeding out next to you, you'd call an ambulance. This is an emergency!

But we don't do that with emotional trauma. We're all out here, bleeding out emotionally in one way or another. And instead of responding with the same urgency as we do for a physical emergency, we tell folks to suck it up.

"Don't cry."

We have an unrealistic expectation of what it means to return to life, love, work, and our families after a traumatic event. We don't have any healthy examples to follow when it comes to making a full recovery from one of these events, so we carry the guilt with us as we try to get back to normal as soon as we can.

If we're lucky (and I use the word "lucky" loosely here), we start learning how to cope in healthy ways at an early age. In a dream world, our parents have done the work and can identify signs of trauma in our behavior and reactions when we're young. If we're lucky, they teach us how to cope in healthy ways and how to process, feel, and express emotions with clarity. How many parents do you know who have done and are doing the work? How was your relationship with your parents? If you had a hard childhood, have you faced that and worked through it? If you can't face your own trauma, how are we going to help the folks closest to us through theirs without projecting our own fears and insecurities onto them? Honestly, most of the weight in my backpack was something *someone else* was scared of that I internalized as my own fear. Now that I have that awareness, it's on me to do the work to unlearn those fears and understand how they've impacted my life. However, it is not my fault that I observed and learned these things at a very young age. Children are brilliant, and for the first several years we're on this planet, we're a sponge for our surroundings.

If you aren't blessed with a family who has done the work and can help you cope, maybe traditional clinical therapy methods are an option. Even so, bad therapists are a thing. It can take some time to find one that you feel comfortable sharing with, and that's assuming you even have a choice.

Adverse reactions and side effects of medications are also an issue. Pharmaceutical therapies come with so many side effects these days, I often wonder if they're helping or hurting us. My friend Chris, the veteran who took his own life at the beginning of 2014, had recently been to the VA and they were adjusting the dosing on his PTSD medication. It is possible that his suicide was tied to the dosing of the medication, a side effect of the drug. We shouldn't live in a world where that is even a remote possibility. The medications that are supposed to help you should not come with side effects like suicidal tendencies or death.

Traditional therapy methods and medications aren't accessible to everyone, so what else can we do?

We aren't naturally equipped to know how to handle this, and few of us ever learn how. We have to start treating mental wellness with the same urgency we do our physical wellness. Until then, our trauma will continue to manifest as mental and physical diseases, and we will continue to be plagued by things that wouldn't stand a chance of harming us as much as they do if we weren't so afraid to talk about them.

That's the thing about trauma. It's so taboo in this society. We demonize it, weaponize it, and it is killing us.

For years, I assumed I was broken, that I was the only one feeling these things, experiencing these thoughts. TV shows, movies, books, they all confirmed my broken-ness. It wasn't until I started sharing these stories with close friends that I realized that I wasn't alone.

Before I could even think about talking to my friends about it, however, I had to talk to myself about it. I had to get to the point where I could even admit that I was raped. I had done such a good job of slut-shaming myself that it took hearing other friends speak about the most violent moments of their lives before I could even wrap my head around what happened to me.

I had to reckon with my own shame and denial, my own internalized misogyny, my own prejudices and biases to realize that I was a victim of a crime. Once I admitted that to myself, then I could start the transition from being in complete denial to understanding why what happened to me wasn't my fault. With that, came unpacking the negative self-talk. Once I realized that my struggles with body image, weight loss, and unhealthy coping mechanisms were beliefs, fears, and behaviors that I adopted when I was a child, and then later in life in a state of trauma, I could start to define a life for myself. I could reclaim my power. I hated the idea of being a victim. Being a survivor felt like a more accurate description.

When I claimed my status as a *survivor* of sexual assault, I felt like anything was possible. If I could navigate life in a trauma-induced haze as well as I had for the past 12 years, what was possible when I had a full understanding of myself? What was possible when I understood my triggers? What was possible if I was brave enough to remove myself from the comfort of the struggle? What was possible if I believed the hype?

I do believe we're all wearing one of these backpacks, and we're all carrying different things. Sexual assault isn't the only kind of trauma, and I hope that piece of trauma isn't in your backpack. However, considering that someone is sexually assaulted every 73 seconds in America, there's a good chance you are carrying this too. Maybe in your pack, it's the weight of your lived experience - racism, sexism, homophobia, transphobia, fatphobia, ableism, and the crimes that stem from those fears, insecurities, and projections. Divorce, separation, breakups and infidelity are traumatic events. Maybe you lost a friend, sibling, loved one or child to gun violence, or perhaps you survived a shooting. If you served in the military, you have had to make choices on behalf of our country that I can't begin to fathom, and the weight of protecting an entire nation is a heavy load to carry. Perhaps it's taking care of your parents or other loved ones. Maybe you witnessed or survived domestic violence. It could be losing a child, loved one, family member, or friend – whether that's a freak accident, a terminal illness, or natural causes. It could be bullying, narcissistic abuse, fertility troubles, manipulative partners or family members, or hostile work environments with inconsiderate colleagues.

When we kill the stigma that trauma makes us broken and start to identify trauma as evidence of common ground, we can move mountains. This is a trail we can and should be walking together.

I'm not saying we should celebrate our shared trauma, and we certainly don't want to dwell in it, but at its very core, it shows us how similar our struggles are. Since everyone has trauma, and trauma isn't a competition, it should be abundantly clear: We are all more alike than different.

When we start prioritizing our emotional trauma with the same urgency we do for physical trauma, we can make significant shifts in how we see ourselves, show up for ourselves, and how we show up in our communities; both locally and globally.

GET OUTSIDE

I tried healing myself physically in a gym, it didn't work. I figured I was a Division 1 athlete in college, I'll just do what I did then, and apply that workout style to my adult life. I'm sorry, do you have six hours a day to work out at a gym? I sure don't. And even when I do have that kind of time, I'm not going to the gym, I'm going on a hike. I had to purposefully craft a life that allows me time to be healthy, because the standard path in this country, at least the one I was set forth on, doesn't allow for it.

Let's talk about why the gym isn't my jam. Maybe you love how you feel after a difficult workout, but hate going to the gym too, and if that's the case, maybe this will resonate. How are you supposed to find holistic healing in a fitness center? Assuming you work indoors, this is practically an extension of your office - no fresh air, no natural light - so it doesn't feel like you're changing up the scenery and keeping things fresh.

With folks grunting and dropping weights, that can be triggering for folks who have survived gun violence or have trauma around loud noises. This sends your body into a state of fight or flight. Every time you go to the gym, you jump when someone drops a weight. Of course, you're going to hate going there, even if you love the activities. That doesn't mean you're lazy, that's your body trying to send messages to your brain that there are better ways to get a good workout - ones that don't trigger you.

With the news barking at you about the world melting down before our eyes and every other commercial warning you of what horrific side effects come with the pills they're slinging on TV, it's hard to tap into your inner knowing. It's hard to practice mindfulness when disempowering lyrics are blasting through the speakers. It's hardly an environment for self-care. Why do you think yoga studios, spas, and retreat centers feel so peaceful and inviting while most gyms feel cold, sterile, and unwelcoming?

Here's the thing though, it doesn't have to be a big adventure to be impactful. You could start with something simple - suggest a walking meeting the next time someone wants to schedule time with you. If you work a desk job, get outside and get some fresh air and find a bench or table to eat your lunch at, away from your screens and away from your desk. Take time to enjoy your food, don't just shovel it into your face like I used to, mindlessly eating fistfuls of snacks while on conference calls because you don't have time to nourish yourself properly.

If you want to go out on a grand adventure, by all means, please do! But know that it can be as simple as walking around your neighborhood and building from there.

Hiking isn't the only activity that can help us find healing in the out-doors, either. In San Diego, I don't like hiking in temperatures higher than 80 degrees so when it's hot, we paddle, and when it's cooler, we hike. You have full permission to try whatever you want, whenever you want, and if you don't like it, that's okay too. You can hike your feelings, run your feelings, paddle your feelings, climb your feelings, bike your feelings, kayak your feelings, backpack your feelings, the list goes on and on.

The common thread between all of these activities is that they happen outside, and they require your full attention. Most of them take you to places where you can disconnect from technology and reconnect with yourself. It's pretty difficult to get stuck in the loop of the mindless scroll through social media when you're solving problems on a rock wall. You're not stuck in front of the TV absorbing negative messaging and advertising when you're in the backcountry on a hike.

WHENEVER YOU CAN, CHOOSE LOVE OVER FEAR

Before I get into this, I want to make this clear. We hear these phrases often, especially in spaces and communities that are intended to promote wellness and healing;

The choice is yours.

Happiness is a choice, so just choose happiness.

Everything is a choice.

All of that is true, but the reason it feels so disingenuous, the reason it feels so floaty and lofty and unattainable is there's never really any substance behind that, at least not from the folks who sell this message in the form of empowerment. There's no acknowledgment that we aren't all born on the same foundation from which to make choices. We don't hold space for different family dynamics, financial situations, community support (or lack thereof), and we lack understanding of other folks' lived experiences.

That's why talking about this is so damn important. If we keep our stories to ourselves, we rob humanity of the opportunity to understand one another. Owning what we've been through, at least with ourselves, is the first step to feeling comfortable talking about it, and the second we let someone else in, as soon as we pass some of our heavy load to someone who is willing and able to help us carry it, we get one step closer to freedom.

When I didn't judge myself in that dressing room in 2016, at the heaviest I'd ever been, I chose love for myself over the fear of being fat, a fear which my mother had instilled in me at a very young age. This was the first domino in my healing journey. After the first hike, my friend Hannah gave me a copy of *Shrill* by Lindy West. Hannah was and still is one of my role models. She is a brilliant woman; smart, kind, no-bullshit, and she's a world-champion skydiver turned Hollywood stuntwoman. She's a legend and was one of the first skydiving coaches I met when I moved to Southern California. When I was training as a competitive skydiver, she was the coach who saw me, who understood me, and who could clearly communicate concepts that I had previously been struggling with. She impacted how I see myself as a skydiver, and how I felt about my body, which my previous coach had told me needed to be under 130 pounds if I ever had a dream of competing at an elite level. My weight felt like a barrier to my success as an athlete. After I found out about his felony convictions, Hannah was the one who scraped me off the proverbial side-walk and helped me navigate all of the toxic things this man had groomed me to believe.

Hannah pointed out all of the women skydivers who had succeeded at a world competition, and a lot of them didn't meet this narrow body standard my coach had given me. As I told her about things that he had said to me over the years, she stopped me dead in my tracks every time and said,

"This is not okay, here is why."

I felt like a child who had zero understanding of what kinds of communication were appropriate and which ones weren't. I was learning all over again, or, more accurately, for the first time. I fancied myself a feminist before I started skydiving, but that chapter of my life had opened up so many learning opportunities and offered so much real-world experience to really come into an understanding of what equality and equity is.

I aspired to have a body like Hannah's - not only because that body met the standards my coach said I needed to meet, but also because she carried herself so confidently, and she went on so many cool adventures. Perhaps most impactful, it appeared to me as if her body didn't get in her way. It didn't hold her back from doing things the way mine did.

So, as I read through *Shrill,* noting Hannah had underlined some surprising passages, I was bewildered. I didn't realize someone who looked like her could also have body image issues. My hatred for my body was visible in how I carried myself and joked about it - my defense mechanism of choice. To see that this woman also had some hang-ups about her own body really opened my eyes.

There is a part of *Shrill* where Lindy West describes "coming out" as fat. She explained, if she owned it, the word couldn't have such a powerful effect on her when she heard it. This single passage in this book was a massive shift in understanding for me. I had always been afraid of being fat, and that word carried so much power for me.

Before the first hike, I diversified who I followed on Instagram and started to see different bodies, ones that weren't only thin white women. As I saw women of all shapes and sizes and colors posting their favorite pictures of themselves, feeling themselves, rocking the world in ways only they knew how, I widened my own definition of beauty. When I saw how many different ways one could be "beautiful" and I saw that some of the bodies looked more like mine, I stopped hating my body so much. Stopping the hate was not the same as loving, but it was a great start.

The first hike taught me I love my body, but I want to be clear, that didn't solve all the problems, reverse years of habits of hating myself, or seal the deal on self-love. In fact, the love I had for my body wasn't its *appearance*, but what it could *do*. This body I didn't recognize back in that dressing room wasn't one that I felt at home in yet, but I didn't hate it.

After that first hike, I gave myself a coming-out party - I was fat. What did I want to do about that? Well, diabetes came along and then I had my answer; it was time to take control of my health. I was stoked that I was comfortable in my body and that I had started to love the skin I was in. It made the transition into managing a chronic illness much easier than if I was still in the throes of self-hatred.

After the second hike, I truly did find love for my body, because I finally had context for why it had "betrayed" me after the assault - holding on to the weight no matter what I fed it or how I moved it. My body hadn't betrayed me, after all. It was sending up warning signs, smoke signals, carrier pigeons, and finally, the last siren, a diabetes diagnosis. This was my body calling out to my brain - HEY DOWN HERE, PAY ATTENTION TO ME. Luckily, I was able to hear the call and I was equipped to answer the phone.

It felt like I was missing something on the body acceptance piece, and this book helped me connect those final dots. When we talk about self-love, body positivity and all of that, the conversation is incomplete. Yes, we should all aim to squash the narrow beauty standards we've been living in and with for the sake of our mental, physical, and emotional health. Yes, we should love the skin we're in, and be comfortable expressing ourselves and taking up space in this world. AND ALSO, once we get away from this deeply rooted hatred for our bodies and move into acceptance, the journey doesn't stop there.

My issues with my body were always centered around acceptance from other folks, but if I take that a step further, if I dig for the root of that belief, what did I really want? I wanted access. I wanted to feel loved. I wanted to feel beautiful. I wanted to feel like I was welcome at the cool kids' table. I wanted to feel like I belonged to something. With these blinders on - this deeply held belief that I wasn't worthy until I was thin - I felt like the *only* thing in my way of having everything I wanted was this body. I felt like my body betrayed me. More than that, I felt like I couldn't control my body, and in a state of trauma, all I wanted was control. I was living in a body that, no matter what I fed it or how I moved it, wouldn't release the weight of my trauma. That was my story until I faced the trauma head-on.

When I chose to aggressively manage my Type 2 Diabetes with diet and exercise, quitting two jobs in the process, I chose love for myself over the fear of the stigma of having the disease, or the fear of the prognosis if I left it untreated.

I'm happy to say that in choosing love for myself in this particular instance, I was able to reverse my Type 2 Diabetes. That sounds like a nice little soundbite, an incredible achievement, and it is. Full stop. But I would be remiss if we didn't discuss just how political this disease is, and how we set people up for failure in their attempts to manage it. My Type 2 diabetes is in remission, made possible because I chose *me*. This disease won't manage itself. I can't cut it out of me. I have to choose myself and my health every day. Sometimes it's easy. Sometimes it's exhausting. Ultimately, this disease is a result of my choices: past, present, and future. It's taken a long time for me to be okay with that. Especially the past part. I am the one who puts food in my mouth. I am the one who decides if and how to move my body. I am the one who manages my stress. Nobody else can do those things for me. This disease is the ultimate test of my ability to understand, articulate, and prioritize my needs. This disease is political, no matter how you slice it; 49% of US adults are pre-diabetic or living with Type 2 Diabetes. This is an epidemic. It's a crisis. And it's 100% preventable, but not without some incredibly hard work.

While it's true that my health is my responsibility, it's also true that there are a variety of systems and societal norms that make it difficult. Not everyone has access to fresh, whole foods. Not everyone has access to medical care. Not everyone has access to emotional support. Not everyone has access to outdoor spaces where healing is possible. Not everyone has time to prioritize their health because we've all been sold a craptastic bill of goods:

We are told that on the other side of hard work is happiness, so we kill ourselves doing work that doesn't accommodate for living life RIGHT NOW.

We are told that on the other side of "get a hot body" is worthiness, so we kill ourselves trying to get smaller to meet some standard set by those who want our money more than our wellness.

And we are told that the most important thing on this planet is to make money. Lots of it. We are all hoarders. Some of us have a house full of material things we can't let go of. Some of us hoard trauma and pass it down generation after generation, without doing the work. Some of us hoard green paper. We accumulate and consume and acquire and exploit each other, the land, and ourselves.

For what? A house? Nice clothes? A fancy car?

What about our health? What about our community?

When I was first diagnosed, I felt so much shame. Once I learned that my choices were what got me here, I felt sick to my stomach. I had brought this upon myself, and it was up to me to fix it. The shame is designed to keep us down. The shame is an intentional weapon deployed by society to keep folks sick, paying big money for drugs, and stockpiling prescriptions to prevent the other side effects. It's bullshit and it has to stop.

Let's talk about how many things are stacked against us in this society and use my privilege as an example of how political this disease truly is.

When I was diagnosed, I was making $118,000 per year, working in corporate America as a marketing director at a prestigious marketing/communications agency. I had the best benefits package available to me through my employer. I lived in San Diego, and I worked from home. I didn't have "let's go buy a boat" money, but we weren't struggling. Anything and everything I needed, within reason, I could purchase.

I worked from home, so I could, within reason, set my own schedule around what meetings I had on the calendar and how heavy my workload was. I was able to wake up early and go for a walk every morning around my neighborhood and paddleboard in the afternoon. I was fortunate that my boss was a compassionate individual who understood that I'd need to be in and out of work to manage this disease effectively. Since I was salaried, I didn't miss a paycheck for taking time off to manage my health.

We lived in a major metropolitan area that made eating healthy as easy as humanly possible. There is a huge selection of vegetarian, gluten-free and vegan options at the restaurants in this town. Between farmer's markets, regular grocery stores, and specialty organic markets, I had seemingly unlimited access to healthy food. I was blessed with a family that prioritized cooking at home and I took a liking to cooking at a very young age, so I knew how to nourish myself and prepare it at home.

My benefits package was top-notch, and there were not a lot of out of pocket expenses after my diagnosis. My frequent labs and doctor visits were all covered with minimal copay, but even if there were expenses, I was making money, and I could have afforded it.

And when I knew I couldn't do this any longer and I quit my first job, I was fortunate that I had another job to go to, even if I was taking a considerable pay cut to work there. When I left the startup, I didn't have much savings to speak of, I didn't have another job lined up, but I did have credit cards with lots of available credit, enough to float us for at least six months if I only made minimum payments, before we had to start making money again. Was that the wisest financial plan? Of course not, but when faced with 95 days of panic attacks, rising blood sugar, and feeling like I was at risk of reversing the progress I had made on managing the disease thus far, it was a no brainer. I'm smart. I'm educated. I'm well-connected. I could always find a job that would help me pay down the debt quickly.

If any of those things weren't true for me, this would have been a very different situation.

If I had to work three jobs and didn't have time for exercise, or if I lived in a food desert and didn't have access to whole, fresh foods, if I didn't have health insurance, if my boss was an asshole and saw my absences as a nuisance rather than encouraging me to do whatever I needed to do to manage my health, I don't know how far along I'd be in working to reverse this disease.

My privilege is only one part of the equation. Let's talk about what else is stacked against us here.

We live in a society that prioritizes work above all else, and this is by design. The American Dream is actually a fantasy, designed by a variety of corporations to keep you striving for things that don't really bring any value to your life. It's not a coincidence that the dream sold to us is measured in material goods: fast car, big house, all the toys (for grownups and children alike).

We work ourselves to death - either in pursuit of this dream if we have the means to access the things we've been conditioned to believe we want (cars, houses, boats, planes, designer handbags, etc.), or because we are working multiple jobs to keep food on the table and a roof over our heads.

Where is the American Dream that shows us living in community with one another, spending time outdoors, caring for our planet, nourishing ourselves with whole foods, having clean water to drink, prioritizing our mental, physical, and spiritual health? Where is the commercial about that? Where are the magazine ads about that?

A self-sufficient population is difficult to control, manipulate, and sell to. So, the cycle continues, and those who dare to see the world differently are cast out, and the ones who can't make ends meet are in a perpetual loop of struggle and trying to catch up. We are so far removed from what we actually need to survive in this world because we are in this constant pursuit of acquiring more: more stuff, more money, more land. This has been happening since the Europeans came to America and started to colonize this country. They boasted of bringing medicine and industry to the Native Americans, but what we really brought was disease, dysfunction, and trauma to the folks who didn't look, love, live, or work like them.

We live in a society where it is so easy to eat poorly. Food completely devoid of nutritional value is easy, accessible, and cheap. And it's designed to be addictive.

In 2013, the New York Times writer Michael Moss interviewed Steven A. Witherly [1], a food scientist and the author of "Why Humans Like Junk Food". In the article, Witherly explained that nacho cheese Doritos are the archetype of addictive processed foods.

They've been engineered so you never feel like you've had enough. Here's why:

The chips have the powerful savory flavor known as umami, as well as what Witherly calls "long hang-time flavors" like garlic that create a lingering smell that stimulates memories. According to Witherly, the recipe balances these powerful tastes so well that no single flavor overpowers and lingers in the mind after you've eaten a chip. This avoids what scientists call "sensory specific satiety" or the feeling of fullness caused by a dominant flavor.

Our food is *engineered* to keep us coming back for more. Look at the price of a bag of chips versus an avocado and it's not hard to see why we make the choices we do.

We live in a society that expects women to care for everyone around them before they care for themselves, while also preaching independence. This society also defines beauty as thin, white, heterosexual, cisgender, and able-bodied. Anything that falls outside of that very narrow standard is tossed aside. Think about it. Think of how hard we work, as women, to take up less space. To be as small as possible. To choose everything and everyone before we choose ourselves. We're told that being selfish is the ultimate sin because nobody likes someone who likes themselves that much. We interpret confidence as arrogance and the effects of doing so are staggering. I was told at a very young age that I'm "too much" and this was confirmed later in my career, over and over and over. While everyone told me I was too much, I never felt like "enough" - I didn't measure up to this standard of beauty. The cognitive dissonance was deafening. For me to be fully expressed, for me to prioritize myself, for me to advocate for my best interests - in my health, in love, and in my career - didn't feel safe.

We live in a society that paints what it means to be a man with a toxic brush - be strong, be a provider, don't show your emotions, make sure you are the head of the household. These expectations manifest in all kinds of ways - violence, projected insecurities when you don't meet the narrow standards of what it means to be a successful man in this society, and entitlement to women's bodies, as evidenced by the statistics surrounding sexual assault, domestic violence, and homicide rates.

We talk about these choices we've made that got us to this place, but we don't hold space for the fact that we aren't all equipped or able to make healthy choices. So, if you're struggling - with anything - and someone tells you should have chosen better, don't let it stop there. Don't succumb to the words and shame that surrounds them. Know that there are a lot of factors outside of your control, and then do what you can to regain control in the areas you can.

Only you know what you're truly up against. Only you know what you can change. But here's a spoiler alert - there's nobody coming in to swoop you up and save you. You have to do this *for* yourself, *by* yourself, AND be willing to accept help from the people who care about you.

Finally, whenever I share my story on tour, as well as with the writing of this book, I'm choosing love for myself over the fear of what happens when a woman stands up and speaks her truth.

Let's face it. Talking about these kinds of topics is still taboo in most of our society. What happens when women stand up and speak their truth? They are chastised, bullied, shamed, and some are even driven to suicide.

What can we do to swing the pendulum in the other direction?

First of all, let's assume the survivor is telling the truth. Instead of putting the burden of proof on the survivor, the person who has survived the most violent act that can be perpetrated against the human body short of murder, let us, if only for a moment, assume they have survived what they say they have survived. That is an incredible feat in and of itself. Rape is an epidemic in this country - someone is sexually assaulted every 73 seconds (RAINN). Survivors of sexual assault are 10 times more likely to attempt suicide than those who haven't experienced sexual assault.[2]

Second, let's cast aside any immediate reaction to assume that survivors are speaking up to ruin the lives of the people who committed the crime. To live through the assault itself, to survive the aftermath, and to arrive at a place where you feel comfortable talking about it in a society that slut-shames victims as a default, is a heroic moment.

I was a student on track to go to medical school, become a surgeon, and save lives. While I certainly wouldn't call the life I've created from the ashes a waste of my time or talent, I know I'm lucky. I'm lucky that I've been able to take what was the most debilitating moment of my life and turn it around into a powerful force for change. Not everyone is equipped to do so. And when I think about that, I think of the lost potential out there.

How many survivors are still being crushed by the weight of this trauma? How many survivors weren't able to complete their education, or even worse, never had a shot at getting an education to begin with? How many are struggling today, under-employed, unable to hold a job, unable to see a healthy way out of the pain? How many are still numbing themselves?

The thought of how many dreams have gone unrealized is paralyzing. What if I hadn't ever found the words to describe what happened to me? What if I didn't ever expand my definition of sexual assault to include a description of my rape? For more than eleven years, I assumed what happened to me was my fault, that I asked for it, all because I wasn't in a dark alley with a stranger putting a gun to my head as it was happening.

The only folks who benefit from our silence are the ones who perpetrated these crimes against our bodies. Literally, nobody else benefits.

First of all, we don't benefit from staying quiet. When we carry this by ourselves, our bodies work in mysterious ways to keep us safe and numb - mine offered up eating and drinking my feelings as my coping mechanisms of choice when I didn't get help.

Our partners don't benefit from our silence. After surviving any kind of trauma, particularly sexual assault, it can be difficult to see a path to healthy love. For years after my assault, I made questionable relationship choices, all in the name of feeling in control. If I was choosing them, then I was empowered, and in some cases, that couldn't have been further from the truth.

When I found out that my boyfriend was married, I stuck around. I didn't value myself enough to see that I was worthy of more, but I felt empowered to make the choice to stay, to stick it out because I was enamored with what we could have been.

When I marched into a bar in Chicago wearing sweatpants, a hoodie, and some knockoff Ugg boots and pointed out the man I was going to take home that night, I didn't value myself enough to see that I was desperate for human touch, but I felt empowered because I made the choice of who touched me.

Society, our communities, the world around us doesn't benefit from our silence.

I didn't tell anyone after my assault and trying to carry that load alone distracted me from my studies. Looking back, I wouldn't change anything that happened to me, not even that morning, because I love where I am right now. But I do think about how many lives I could have saved as a surgeon. Maybe I would have found a cure for cancer. Maybe I would have invented some revolutionary procedure or technique that could have changed the way we approach medicine. I'm lucky that my pivot in my studies took me where it did, and that I'm able to share this story with you now. I'm lucky that my aftermath was largely academic, and not the gateway to more trauma.

Because trauma is the gateway drug. Read that again.

Every night that I had too much to drink and insisted on driving home intoxicated, I didn't value myself enough to dig to the root of that. I didn't want to see that the last time I *didn't* drive home drunk, when I followed my friend's pleas to stay at their house, I was raped. In the aftermath of my assault, driving home in various states of intoxication felt like I had chosen my safety, even if I was in no condition to drive. If something happened to me, at least it would be my choices that got me there, not at the hands of someone taking advantage of me.

I'm fortunate that my numbing stopped at alcohol and ice cream, that it didn't extend to harder substances like opiates, heroin, cocaine, or methamphetamines.

Our families don't benefit from our silence. I grew up in a tight-knit Midwestern household. We told each other everything, but I couldn't tell them this. After I got done with the second hike and I shared the discoveries I had made on-trail with my family, I felt a negative shift in our family dynamic. My father, who I grew up with as my best friend, seemed to change within seconds.

This is heavy stuff and I expected a reaction, but this was not the reaction I expected. After I finished sharing about what had happened, he cut me off, going on to say that my story was bullshit and I better come up with a new one, because nobody is buying the story I'm telling. I quickly got acquainted with establishing boundaries, because growing up, I had none.

Through shared stories and a handful of "ah-ha" moments, it became abundantly clear to me – this is generational trauma.

Trauma can be generational, and it gets passed down again and again through our silence. Our bodies retain it, store it, and know it. And it's not until someone decides to disrupt the pattern, to take their trauma into their own hands, examine it, work through it, and do the hard work to heal, that the cycle stops.

If trauma can be passed down generation to generation, so can healing.

Would I have been raped if our family had spoken more openly about sexual violence? Maybe. Maybe not. But I know that by sharing my experiences, I am able to give folks language that may help them articulate what happened to them, which is the first step to the healing process.

So, if you're reading this and you've survived some hard things, hi. Welcome to the next chapter of your life. If you've found some of your story within these pages, know that it's because we're way more alike than we are different. I'm sorry if my words have caused you pain, but the fact that you're able to feel is one of the most beautiful parts of the human experience. There is no shame in crying, screaming, and curling up in the fetal position. I won't take it personally if my story stirs up feelings in you that are terrifying and make you want to burn this book.

I will say this: I believe you. I see you. I love you. I hear you. We got this.

Also, trauma isn't a competition. If you're reading this and comparing your story to mine, thinking that you've survived more or less, please stop yourself. What is true for you is true for you, full stop. You get to define your trauma. You get to claim the parts of your story you've been scared to claim. You get to decide how you show up, how you heal, and how you move forward in this world. I don't get to do that for you. Your family doesn't get to do that for you. Neither do your friends, colleagues, medical professionals, coaches, or teachers. Only you can decide what you're ready to reclaim. Only you can decide what that looks like.

And if there's a chance you're like me, I need you to hear this loud and clear: if you have been reading this, nodding a lot, and you feel like my story is your story - that's because it is. We are all one. We are all part of a collective consciousness. Unity is power. Our lived experiences are ours and are unique to us, but the major through lines of our stories are shared. Whether you believe in the Universe, God, unicorns, the flying spaghetti monster or anything in between - at the end of the day, we are all mirrors for each other. If you're inspired and want to aspire to find this kind of healing, to know yourself this well, all you have to do now is to recognize that you are worthy of embodying these qualities. You recognize these qualities in me and the other people you look up to because you already hold them within yourself.

You can do this. Together, *we* can do this. And know this much; I've got your back.

:)

You only get so
many sunsets.

PROMPTS FOR REFLECTION

This is a self-help book in that there isn't anything I've done here that you can't do for your*self*. As I mentioned at the beginning, I'm not a doctor, nor am I a therapist, so take what works for you and leave the rest.

While I wish I had access to traditional therapy methods and professionals who can help me sort through my past, and while I wish I had gotten help after my assault, I didn't. Everything I was able to discover throughout this process was thanks to my journaling practice and spending time away from all the influences that tell me I'm not enough or that I'm too much.

For me, that's hiking. Maybe you have a different activity of choice like rock climbing, running, kayaking, fishing, gardening, riding your bike, or paddleboarding. Perhaps you're where I was back in 2016, ass firmly planted on the couch, but knowing you're ready to take the next step.

My journaling practice wasn't always something that I did every day, but when I felt called to write or when I wanted to make sure I remembered what was happening in my life, I made time to journal. As I got started back up after my hiatus, it was sporadic. As work got busy, I didn't prioritize journaling. As work calmed down, I made more time. The key for me was to just do it when I wanted to do it, and not have an expectation or assumption that it was *only* beneficial if I did it every day.

As time went on, I got protective of my journaling time. It was time for me to reflect, to process, to take the time I needed, uninterrupted, to find my thoughts. Soon enough, if I went a few days without journaling, I felt like my brain was cluttered, and I'd write furiously trying to remember what had happened in the days between entries, trying to organize my thoughts. I loved how I felt after I got everything out of my head and into the journal, and I wanted more of that feeling, so my practice became more and more regular.

A lot of folks prescribe journaling every day, dumping 10 minutes of free writing every single morning. And for some folks, that's attainable. For some of us, writing, journaling, and otherwise spending time with our thoughts can be a scary process. It can be terrifying to get to the place where we aren't distracted, where our thoughts have room to breathe without interruption.

Give yourself permission to do this as often as you'd like, and if it gets hard, give yourself the grace to take a break. This isn't a race. We have the rest of our lives to unpack our traumapacks.

When you're ready, take a minute to read, sit with, and respond to these prompts. I highly recommend preparing your space, having a glass of water, coffee, tea – whatever makes you feel cozy and at home, and gifting yourself the time to do these at whatever pace you like.

This is your journey, you set the schedule.

CHAPTER 1

✓ Who have I lost in my life?

_____

_____

_____

✓ What did they mean to me?

_____

_____

_____

_____

✓ What is my favorite memory of them?

_____

_____

_____

_____

✓ Is there anyone I know who I could call to share this memory with today?

_____

_____

_____

_____

CHAPTER 2

✓ When was the last time I decided to do something I didn't know I could do?

_____

_____

_____

✓ Is there anything I've been putting off until I meet some arbitrary standard? (Example: I put off so many things "until I lost weight" - like events, spending time on the beach, enjoying intimacy)

_____

_____

_____

_____

✓ Where did I learn this standard?

_____

_____

_____

_____

CHAPTER 3

✓ When was the last time I tried something for the first time?

_____

_____

_____

✓ How did I feel before I did it?

_____

_____

_____

✓ How did it feel to do it?

_____

_____

_____

✓ How do I feel about that experience now?

_____

_____

_____

_____

CHAPTER 4

✓   If you have a partner: Do you remember the day you met?
Write about that day in as much detail as you can.

_____

_____

_____

_____

_____

_____

_____

_____

_____

_____

_____

_____

_____

_____

_____

_____

✓ If you don't have a partner but would like to have one some-day: Imagine you're in a safe, loving, committed relationship. Write your story. How did you meet? What qualities does your partner possess? How do they challenge you to be a better person?

_____

_____

_____

_____

_____

✓ If you don't have a partner and you're happy solo: What is one way you can do something nice for yourself today? How can you validate yourself?

_____

_____

_____

_____

✓ Has anything happened that was definitely not funny at the time that I can laugh at now?

_____

_____

_____

CHAPTER 5

✓ Have you ever thought you couldn't do something and then
set out to prove yourself wrong? How did it feel to accom-
plish that thing?

_____

_____

_____

✓ Take the same scenario or think of a big goal you're considering pursuing. Does it feel different to assume you can
do it, and then set out to prove yourself right? What does
that feel like?

_____

_____

_____

_____

✓ What is an activity you do every day that is repetitive? Can
you pick a mantra to say while doing it?

_____

_____

_____

_____

_____

✓ Have you thanked your body for how it works for you today? This week? This month? The past year? Even if it feels scary, unsafe, or foreign to think of our bodies in this way, if you're reading this, you're alive. Start there.

_____

_____

_____

_____

_____

_____

✓ Is there a part of your body that causes you anxiety or shame? What is one thing you could do to build a loving relationship with that part of your body?

_____

_____

_____

_____

_____

_____

CHAPTER 6

✓ When was the last time you sat in silence without distractions? When was the last time you spent more than two days away from your phone?

_____

_____

✓ If you've never spent time away from your phone, social media, emails, etc, is it possible that you're trying to distract yourself from something? (NOTE: the first thing that comes to mind is usually exactly what's happening, good or bad. We can distract ourselves when feelings are scary, and we can distract ourselves from success if we're on the brink of a breakthrough or major shift.)

_____

_____

_____

✓ When was the last time you asked your body what it needs? Have you ever given it a chance to answer?

_____

_____

_____

_____

CHAPTER 7

✓ Where were you the last time you got shocking news? What do you remember from that day?

_____

_____

_____

✓ If you're living with pre-diabetes or Type 2 Diabetes, what actions are you taking every day to manage the disease?

_____

_____

_____

✓ If you're currently trying to manage your physical weight, how are you managing your emotional, mental, and spiritual well-being?

_____

_____

_____

✓ Are there any stories you're telling yourself that you'd like to release? What would it feel like to let go of them?

_____

_____

_____

CHAPTER 8

✓ If you are a survivor of sexual assault, have you come to terms with what happened to you? Have you told someone you trust?

_____

_____

_____

RESOURCE: If you want to talk to someone who can help, call RAINN at 1-800-656-4673 or visit RAINN.org

✓ When you hear the phrase "the choice is yours" or "everything is a choice" – how does that make you feel?

_____

_____

_____

_____

✓ Are there chapters of your life you'd like to reclaim as your own? Have you lost touch with certain aspects of yourself that you'd like to re-integrate?

_____

_____

_____

_____

CHAPTER 9

✓ If you're employed, describe your first day at your current job.

_____

_____

_____

✓ If you're not employed and are seeking work: what is your dream job? What does your first day at your dream job feel like? What is the work environment like (outside, indoors, at a desk, in an office, at a store, etc)? What do you wear on your first day? What do you eat for lunch?

_____

_____

_____

_____

✓ Have you ever been passed on for an opportunity at work that you definitely could have exceeded at? How did that make you feel? Where do you feel that feeling in your body?

_____

_____

_____

_____

CHAPTER 10

✓ Have you ever had an emotional reaction at work or school that you weren't proud of? Looking back, what would you do differently?

_____

_____

_____

_____

✓ When was the last time you clearly articulated your needs, without fear of what would happen next?

_____

_____

_____

✓ Who is on your personal board of directors? When you have a big decision to make, who do you consult? Who is your first call? Have you called them to say thank you lately?

_____

_____

_____

_____

_____

CHAPTER 11

✓ When was the last time you prioritized your health over everything else on your to-do list?

_____

_____

_____

_____

✓ How do you cope when you're stressed out? How do you celebrate?

_____

_____

_____

_____

✓ When you're feeling stressed, where do you feel it in your body?

_____

_____

_____

_____

CHAPTER 12

✓ If you knew you were going to die tomorrow, what would you want the people closest to you to know? Regardless of whether they're dead or alive, what would you say to your

◊ Mother
◊ Father
◊ Siblings
◊ Extended family
◊ Partner
◊ Best friend
◊ Boss/Teacher/Coach

_____

_____

_____

_____

_____

_____

_____

_____

_____

_____

_____

_____

✓ Can you think of someone who has impacted your life in a positive way? Have you told them how they've impacted you? If not, let them know!

_____

_____

_____

_____

_____

_____

_____

✓ When you're dead, what do you want people to remember about you?

_____

_____

_____

_____

_____

_____

_____

CHAPTER 13

✓ In general, do you assume things will go well or go poorly?

_____

_____

_____

✓ If you've lost children, friends, family, or colleagues, did you give yourself space to grieve? Are you still grieving? What kind of support would feel good to you?

_____

_____

_____

✓ When was the last time you felt comfortable in your skin? Where were you? What were you doing? Who were you with? What did it feel like?

_____

_____

_____

_____

RESOURCES: _The Desire Map by Danielle LaPorte - this is the book/workbook I used to get in touch with my core desired feelings._

CHAPTER 14

✓ When was the last time you assumed something would go wrong, but instead it went very right?

_____

_____

_____

✓ Set a goal for yourself and get specific - how do you feel in pursuit of the goal? How do you feel once you've achieved it. Visualize your success.

_____

_____

_____

_____

✓ When was the last time you played like a kid?

_____

_____

_____

_____

_____

CHAPTER 15

✓ What are things about your body that people (or the media you consume) have told you are bad or wrong that you've been trying to fix?

_____

_____

_____

_____

✓ Are there parts of your body you'd like to reclaim?

_____

_____

_____

_____

✓ Can you hype yourself up?

_____

_____

_____

_____

CHAPTER 16

✓ Do you have a negative internal soundtrack? What are some of the things you hear?

_____

_____

_____

✓ When you hear these things, who is saying it? Is it your voice or someone else's?

_____

_____

_____

✓ What would it feel like to release those beliefs? What if they didn't have power over you?

_____

_____

_____

✓ Can you hype yourself up here, too?

_____

_____

_____

CHAPTER 17

✓ Think back to the last time you felt on fire - like everything was aligned. What happened after that?

_____

_____

_____

_____

_____

✓ When was the last time you stood in awe of your body and what it can do?

_____

_____

_____

✓ Do you believe in something bigger than yourself? What is it?

_____

_____

_____

_____

CHAPTER 18

✓ What is a heavy thing in your traumapack?

_____

_____

_____

✓ Is it yours or are you carrying it for someone else?

_____

_____

_____

✓ For the things that aren't yours, how does it feel to know that you don't have to carry it?

_____

_____

_____

_____

✓ Think about the last major decision you made, did you make that decision from a place of love or a place of fear?

_____

_____

_____

_____

✓ Family stories can be heavy - when you think of what you have survived, has anyone in your family had a similar experience? How have they dealt with it?

_____

_____

_____

_____

_____

✓ Revisiting the stories we tell ourselves - is there anything else you'd like to release?

_____

_____

_____

_____

_____

_____

_____

_____

_____

SUPPORT
RESOURCES

If you or someone you know is a survivor of sexual assault, is having suicidal thoughts, or is concerned about their risk factors for diabetes and are in need of support, the following organizations are a great place to start:

1 **RAINN**
- Call 1-800-656-4673
- Visit rainn.org

2 **National Suicide Prevention Lifeline**
- Call 1-800-273-8255
- Visit suicidepreventionlifeline.org/

3 **American Diabetes Association**
- Visit Diabetes.org

HIKING MY FEELINGS RESOURCES

There's more where this came from. Check out the following ways to stay connected, continue the conversation, and find more resources for your journey:

- Book resources and exclusive content: hikingmyfeelings.com/book
- Catch us on the road or on the trail: hikingmyfeelings.com/events
- Join one of our Hike + Heal retreats: hikingmyfeelings.com/retreats
- Follow us on Instagram: instagram.com/hikingmyfeelings
- Tag your journey: #hikingmyfeelings

OUTDOOR COMMUNITY RESOURCES

Are you interested in hitting the trail but unsure where to start? Do you feel like you're not outdoorsy, or that people who look, love, or live like you aren't welcome in the outdoors? You're not alone. Below, please find a whole host of communities I love and trust will take good care of you if you join them for an adventure. Some of these organizations have local chapters, some of them are great resources for specific communities in the outdoors, and all of them are ready to welcome you, no matter who you are (assuming you aren't an asshole).

In no particular order, here are some of the communities doing the work to make the outdoors a more inclusive place for everyone. This is by no means an exhaustive list, so be sure to check the resources sections of their websites to be connected even further:

- **Women Who Hike - womenwhohike.com**

Women Who Hike is a worldwide organization that empowers women on and off the trail. Through their online communities and group hikes, you can connect with women who hike all over the world.

- **Outdoor Journal Tour - outdoorjournaltour.com**

The Outdoor Journal Tour is a hybrid health organization that combines the healing tenets of outdoor activity with mindful meditation and introspective journaling. Be sure to check out #WeHikeToHeal – an annual wellness initiative in March to celebrate Women's History Month.

- **Unlikely Hikers - unlikelyhikers.com**

Unlikely Hikers creates a safe, supportive, intentional, body-positive outdoor community for people underrepresented in outdoor culture (people of color, people of size, trans, queer and beyond).

Be sure to check out Jenny's list of plus size outdoor gear - https://jennybruso.com/plussize/

- **Fat Girls Hiking - fatgirlshiking.com**

Fat Girls Hiking is fat activism, body liberation & outdoor community. They aim to take the shame and stigma out of the word FAT and empower it. Their motto, Trails Not Scales focuses on self-care in the outdoors.

- **Outdoor Afro - outdoorafro.com**

The nation's leading, cutting edge network that celebrates and inspires African American connections and leadership in nature. They help people take better care of themselves, our communities, and our planet.

- **Latino Outdoors - latinooutdoors.org**

Their vision is that the diversity of the Latino identity is connected with the diversity of outdoor experiences, and they are active stewards and advocates for our natural spaces, sharing our stories and empowering the next generation of Latino leadership in the outdoors.

- **Venture Out - ventureoutproject.com**

The Venture Out Project is committed to facilitating backpacking and wilderness trips for the queer and trans community in a safe and inclusive environment.

- Indigenous Women Hike - indigenouswomenhike.com

Indigenous Women Hike is an organization striving to increase the visibility of indigenous folks in the outdoors and increase awareness of the first people to live on the land.

REFERENCES

1   Moss, M. (October 1, 2013). *The Nacho Dorito*. Retrieved from https://archive.nytimes.com/www.nytimes.com/interactive/2013/10/01/dining/nacho-graphic.html

2   Kilpatrick, D.G., Edmunds, C.N., & Seymour, A.K. (1992). *Rape in America: A report to the nation*. Arlington, VA: National Victim Center and Medical University of South Carolina.

ABOUT THE AUTHOR

When former collegiate athlete and competitive skydiver, Sydney Williams, unexpectedly found herself on the receiving end of a Type 2 diabetes diagnosis, while grappling with unresolved trauma from a decades-old sexual assault, she set out on a mission: turn her pain into power. Two hikes across Catalina Island and 80 miles later, she founded **Hiking My Feelings**® to help others tap into the mind-body connection and healing power of nature that helped kick her self-limiting beliefs and disease into remission.

Having more than 10 years of marketing experience with Fortune 500 companies and emerging brands, Sydney serves up her "truth juice" style of storytelling to break wide open tough conversations with practical, powerful content and experiences. Over the years, she's been featured on the **SXSW** stage, as well as in *Huffington Post, Psychology Today, US News & World Report*, and numerous other publications. Today, she is the author of *Hiking My Feelings: Stepping Into the Healing Power of Nature* and travels across the country empowering others to summit their personal mountains on their way to becoming Well Beings.

Made in the USA
Las Vegas, NV
20 August 2022